WILD
MOOSE
COUNTRY

Photography © 1998: Robin Brandt: front cover, 11, 20-21, 53, 56-57, 75, 78, 90, 106, 119, 145, 151; Gary Schultz/ The Wildlife Collection: front flap; Steve Maas: 3, 8, 35, 156-157; Len Rue, Jr./Bruce Coleman Inc.: 4-5; Erwin & Peggy Bauer: 7, 44, 62, 63, 66, 69, 92, 114-115, 117, 129, 142, 143; Henry H. Holdsworth/Wild By Nature: 10, 18, 31, 38, 39, 43, 46-47, 49, 50, 61, 70, 72-73, 74, 77, 91, 93, 108, 116, 120, 121, 125, 126, 130, 132-133, 135, 144, 146, 148-149, 154-155; Tom Walker: 13, 64-65, 67; Richard Hamilton Smith: 14, 96; Mark Newman/ Tom Stack & Associates: 16-17, 107, 139; Thomas Kitchin/Tom Stack & Associates: 19, 32-33, 113, 140-141; Mark Raycroft: 22, 27, 36, 41, 100, 104; Robert McCaw: 23, 26; Leonard Lee Rue III: 24-25, 30; Craig Brandt: 28, 37, 52, 58, 59, 76, 89, 101, 105; Charles H. Willey: 34, 48, 51, 54, 55, 60, 85, 95, 118, 134, 147, 152, 153; Wendy Shattil & Bob Rozinski/Tom Stack & Associates: 40, 102-103; Erwin & Peggy Bauer/Bruce Coleman Inc.: 79; Michael H. Francis: 80-81, 83, 98-99; Diana L. Stratton/Tom Stack & Associates: 82; François Gohier: 84; Len Rue, Jr.: 86-87, 88, 122; Wendy Shattil & Bob Rozinski: 109; Victoria Hurst/Tom Stack & Associates: 110; John Shaw/Tom Stack & Associates: 136; W. E. Ruth/Tom Walker, Agent: back cover.

NorthWord Press
5900 Green Oak Drive
Minnetonka, MN 55343
1-800-328-3895

Book design by Russell S. Kuepper

Library of Congress Cataloging-in-Publication Data
Strong, Paul.
      Wild moose country / by Paul Strong.
            p.   cm.
      Includes bibliographical references (p.   ).
      Includes index.
      ISBN 1-55971-638-X (hardcover)
      1. Moose. I. Title.
      QL737.U55S79   1998
      599.65'7—dc21   97-5959

Printed in U.S.A.
02 01 00 99 98 / 1 2 3 4 5

WILD
MOOSE
COUNTRY

Paul Strong

NorthWord Press
Minnetonka, Minnesota

Dedication

To Donna, my partner.

Acknowledgments

Numerous people have contributed to this book, most of them indirectly through their studies and publications. Others have played a more direct part. As always, Barbara Harold has been a thoughtful and patient editor. Maureen McCloskey, Sharon Johnson, and Kathy Tromp, at Nicolet Technical College Library, provided cheerful support in obtaining literature for me and in guiding me through library search procedures. Eunice Padley obtained invaluable library materials for me from the University of Wisconsin.

The Boone and Crockett Club generously provided current world records for moose racks in North America. Bucky Dennerlein with the National Audubon Society's Alaska Regional Office brought me up-to-date on the aerial wolf killing story in Alaska.

Bill "Moose Willie" Faber from the Grimso Wildlife Research Center in Sweden provided information for that country and was invaluable as a source of names and E-mail addresses of other moose biologists in Europe and Asia. Numerous scientists and wildlife managers from around the world provided information about moose in their area including Rob Aho, John Beecham, Jim Bevan, Alan Bisset, Petras Bluzma, Wendy Bolduc, Eduardas Budrys, Rehaume Courtois, Vince Crichton, Adrian D'Hont, Greg Evans, Bill Haggerty, John Hall, Ian Hatter, Jari Heikkila, Al Hicks, Bogumila Jedrzejewska, Jingbo Jia, Sanna-Kaisa Juvonen, John McDonald, Don McKinnon, Brian McLaren, Don Meredith, Anthony Nette, Tuire Nygren, Jim Peek, Gerry Redmond, Erling Solberg, and Susan Westover.

My family endured my erratic schedule, long hours at the computer, and endless stories about moose biology and trivia. For their patience, tolerance, support, and love, I am eternally grateful. Lessons learned from my mother and father continue to provide me with the ability and persistence to carry out such a project as this.

*The Northwoods' monarch —
a bull moose in the prime of life.*

Table of Contents

A young bull in favored wetland habitat.

Preface

Many children growing up in Maine as I did during the 1960s and 1970s had an inbred consciousness of moose even if they had never seen one. The state flag, which flew from most school flagpoles, depicted the state seal, in which a moose is lying down. Despite never seeing a moose until I was a teenager, I knew there had to be moose in Maine just because of that state flag.

During that time, moose were considered to be majestic and mysterious monarchs of the large, unsettled northern part of the state we referred to as the Northwoods. They were to be seen on a rare camping or fishing trip during the summer or by a lucky few in whose town a moose infected with brainworm wandered.

One of those moose passed through my home town in Lincoln County. It happened one day while school was in session, but I wasn't fast enough to the window to see it before it disappeared into the woods. Nor was I lucky enough to be with my father on our property the day a large bull moose wandered into the neighbor's cottage yard. Old Henry Webber, nearly deaf and working in his garage that day, thought the noise was his wife, Edna, calling to him. He turned around and came face to face with the moose. My father still tells the story of Henry's moose, which, after frightening Henry, tromped across the old stone wall to our property and then proceeded to swim a mile across the lake with a brief stop for rest on an island.

I finally saw my first moose on a Boy Scout camping trip to Mt. Katahdin in Baxter State Park around the age of thirteen. That moose was belly-deep in water, pulling up lilies and calmly chewing them as cars stopped along the road and viewers gawked. I later came to see moose almost daily as I conducted scientific studies of loons on several lakes in northern Maine. While their appearance became commonplace, my awe for their sheer size and majesty never faded. I still remember the day my crew and I saw triplet moose calves and the night a cow moose stared intently through my cabin window as I sat reading a book before a flickering gas lantern. Nor can I ever forget a soggy night when the air was so thick with no-see-ums that my friend, Rob Burke, let his dog sleep in our tent. Just before dozing off, we awoke to Jess's muffled woofs followed quickly by a moose running by the tent at full speed, taking down several guy lines in the process.

I don't see many moose these days in northeastern Wisconsin. Moose were here at one time, but had been gone half a century before starting to show up again. Every once in awhile, one wanders down from Michigan's Upper Peninsula and someone spots it. I count my blessings when my business takes me into moose country and I spy one or two as I did one February morning in a grove of aspen next to Route 2 west of Duluth, Minnesota, and another time on the road into Franconia Notch in New Hampshire. We almost clipped that cow moose in New Hampshire with our car. It impressed me—with its size and agility as it ran quickly into a brushy opening and stopped to look back—just as much as the one nearly thirty years ago on that pond in Baxter State Park.

Here, then, is a book about moose and wild moose country for people who already know or want to know and cherish these creatures and their places as much as I do.

CHAPTER ONE

Old Bucketnose

One of the truly remarkable sights for any northern outdoorsperson is a moose lifting its enormous head from a willow thicket or up out of a woodland lake. The largest member of the deer family currently roaming the planet, the moose seems to belong to another size scale of creatures. It so dwarfs its abundant and commonly seen cousins, the white-tailed and mule deer, that hunters, canoeists, and hikers are frequently shocked by its sheer size and bulk. Weighing up to 1,700 pounds and standing nearly seven feet tall at the shoulder, the moose is one of the northern hemisphere's largest land mammals.

Moose differ clearly from other living members of the deer family in several ways. Unlike the more equally proportioned elk and deer, the moose is a top-heavy creature, with the majority of its weight perched atop four seemingly spindly legs. Its pendulous and mobile upper lip gives it a long face ending in a "bucket nose" that is out of proportion to the rest of the body. All moose have a beardlike flap of skin under the chin, called a dewlap or bell. The males carry a set of broad, scooplike antlers that can span five feet from tip to tip and can weigh up to 70 pounds.

The "bucket" nose distinguishes the moose from other members of the deer family.

Anatomically, the moose does not have any known unique features. However, it shares with the oxen an unusual characteristic known as the heart bone. Only discovered recently by Ukrainian scientists, this small bone about one inch long is formed after birth and is located in the area of the heart near the discharge point of the left ventricle. Scientists believe this bone may serve a support and protection role for a large heart weighing up to six pounds.

The beardlike flap beneath the chin is called the bell.

Weight

Like their elk cousins, male moose are called bulls, females are cows, and young are referred to as calves. Bulls and cows are similar in general appearance during the antler-free season, with bulls typically larger. Bulls continue to grow and add weight at least until they are ten years old. Cows reach their maximum weight after four to five years.

There is a great deal of variation in weights of moose across their range and within localized areas. Generally, moose inhabiting lower latitudes are smaller than those of the far north. The smallest races (or subspecies) are found in central Europe and Asia and in the lower 48 United States. A very large Manchurian moose from China tipped the scales at nearly 800 pounds, but most are considerably smaller. Similarly, adult bulls in the mountains of Utah and Wyoming may regularly weigh 750 to 850 pounds. Large bulls from Alaska and Siberia regularly reach 1,500 or more pounds. The largest known moose on record was a mature bull living at the Alaska Department of Fish and Game's Moose Research Center in Soldotna. Named Bando, he reached his greatest weight at 1,693 pounds. If there is a larger moose than Bando out there, it is a safe bet he is a bull about ten years old living out on the Alaskan or Siberian tundra.

Climate, population density, and the ratio of males to females all affect body weight of moose. Studies in Norway and Sweden concluded that bulls were smaller when there was a high population density and when the ratio of bulls to cows was low. Yearling bulls were most affected by climate, growing much faster during cool and dry summers. Cows were largely unaffected by the same factors.

Weight was related to latitude for both adult cows and bulls, with the larger animals living in northern climates. In fact, northern moose weighed 15 to 20 percent more than their southern counterparts. Moose stop growing after they reach a certain age and in the Swedish study, the bulls in northern Sweden reached their maximum weight after six years while cows reached theirs after four. The large size of the bulls was in part determined by two more years of growth than cows. The same pattern was exhibited in southern Sweden, but age at maximum weight was reached earlier by about two years for both sexes.

Clearly, the body weight of any individual moose is controlled by a variety of complex and interrelated factors—gender, heredity, climate, location, food availability, population density, and sex ratio of the population—few of which remain constant over an animal's life.

Pelage

The moose is well adapted to the cold environments it inhabits. Its large body retains heat far better than smaller animals and it is covered with a thick undercoat of dense hair and a second layer of ten-inch-long, hollow guard hairs, which provide excellent insulation. Moose exhibit a range of hair colors. Moose living in the lower 48 United States and Canada typically have dark brown hair all over or dark brown everywhere except the chest and belly, which can be gray. Most moose in Russia have roughly the same coloration. White moose are uncommon, but recorded regularly in parts of Ontario and Manitoba. These moose aren't albinos, but are an unusual color phase.

The one area where hair color is decidedly different is Alaska. There, the pelage varies from dark brown to a grizzled blond and occasionally to white. However, with the exception of the white moose, one characteristic is constant. Almost all Alaskan moose have a band of black hair which extends across the rump and tapers downward along

White moose are not albinos and are observed infrequently.

the sides to the shoulder. The dark hair stands out on the rump and is considered a unique feature to moose in that area. Scientists are unsure of the function of the "rump patch" in Alaskan moose. A reasonable explanation may be that the patch acts as a social signal because these moose occupy a more open habitat on the tundra than most other North American moose of boreal forests, and visual cues may be more important in the social pattern of open-country animals.

Locomotion

The moose's long legs allow it to move through snow up to five or six feet deep. In extremely deep snow conditions, they may kneel and use their forelegs as snowshoes. Typically, cloven hooves and dew claws (vestigial toes above the hooves on the back side of the leg) provide a wide base that adds stability to uneven and unstable footing on snow and in mud, bogs, and lake bottoms. The front hooves are larger than the back ones and bulls have longer hooves than cows. Observant trackers can make an educated guess regarding the sex of the animal based on the shape of the hoof marks. Bulls' tracks are blunter at the front end while cows' tracks have a sharper point. A cow's track has more of an overall circular outline, while those of bulls are more oblong.

Long legs aid locomotion in rugged terrain.

The long legs and higher front than rear pose a problem for a moose wanting to lower its head to feed or drink. When a moose has to reach all the way to its hooves, it either spreads it legs to the sides, puts one foot forward and one backward before bending the knees, or just bends its knees slightly. It may even kneel to reach water or low vegetation.

The typical land gait of moose is a slow plod, although they also trot and can gallop for short periods. Moose are sure-footed and pick their way carefully through muskegs and bogs. On flat terrain, they often trot from site to site at speeds around 6 mph. In a panic, they gallop and have been recorded at speeds of 20 to 35 mph over short distances. Sometimes appearing awkward, moose are remarkably graceful and move through dense forests nimbly and with little sound unless they are running.

Moose are not the athletic jumpers some other hoofed mammals are. They prefer to walk around obstacles or step over them. When pressed, however, they rear up on their hind legs, place their forelegs over the barrier, and leap over. Evidence suggests that they can clear objects up to six feet high.

In the water, moose are strong swimmers and have great endurance. They are capable of speeds up to 15 mph when chased, but typically swim at a more leisurely rate. Instead of walking the shoreline around a lake, a moose will often swim directly across it, sometimes covering over a mile. There are verified records of long-distance swims across large lakes or ocean bays that covered 8 to 12 miles.

I gained personal experience with the speed of swimming moose while conducting wildlife studies in northern Maine in the 1980s. When my colleagues and I saw a moose crossing the lake, we would occasionally motor over for a closer look. Our fourteen-foot Starcraft aluminum v-hull powered by a ten-horse outboard needed more than half throttle to keep up with large bulls. When we were in a canoe, two of us could not keep pace with some adult cows and most of the large bulls.

Moose are not reluctant to become completely submerged when in the pursuit of aquatic plants for food. They may swim out into water up to twenty feet deep before diving. Their average underwater forays last around thirty seconds and they are rarely submerged for more than a minute.

Bell

One of the most striking features of the moose is the beard under the chin, called the bell. It has intrigued people for years and has been recognized by humans through recent history including its depiction in cave paintings in Europe and in pictographs from North American Indians. The bell is found on moose all over the world although there is a great deal of variation in its size and shape. It is nearly absent in Chinese moose and is small in Swedish moose.

The bell is present on both sexes and on calves, although it is so small as to be inconspicuous on young animals. Bells increase in size as animals grow older. Bulls have larger bells than cows of the same age. The shape of the bell in cows is typically a long, narrow tail of hair suspended from a short, fleshy dewlap. The longest tail-like bells are in young bulls from two to four years old. Bulls

in their prime—between five and ten years old—have a large, sac-shaped bell, which may lack a long tail. Apparently, the tail part of the bell is commonly lost through freezing.

The function of the bell is not clear. It is believed to indicate age and sex during the antler-free season, and also plays a role during the breeding season. There is evidence to support the idea that the bell holds chemicals from the bull's urine and saliva that are used in breeding behavior.

Moose Muffle

The snout of a moose undergoes major change from the moose's birth to adulthood. Calves have a relatively short muzzle that measures around a foot at birth. At eight or nine weeks, the muzzle lengthens by several inches. By six months, the muzzle is a half foot longer than at birth, but doesn't reach full development until after one year. At this time, there is a large, overhanging nose and top lip, sometimes referred to as the "moose muffle." Moose muffle stew is considered a delicacy in some northern kitchens.

The lower jaw, short at birth, lengthens rapidly as well until about two-and-a-half years of age to accommodate a mouthful of teeth. Moose have an unusual tooth pattern. They completely lack incisors on their upper jaw and must clip off vegetation with the six lower jaw incisors against the hard palate of the top of the mouth. This often results in less than a neat clip and more tearing of bark and twigs. Canine teeth are absent on the top. There are three premolars and three large molars used for grinding plant material.

Teeth wear down over years of use. Because the efficiency of digestion is so important for moose, when teeth lose their ability to grind plant material effectively, the survival rate of individuals declines. This probably starts around seven to nine years of

Mature bulls grow large, scoop-shaped antlers.

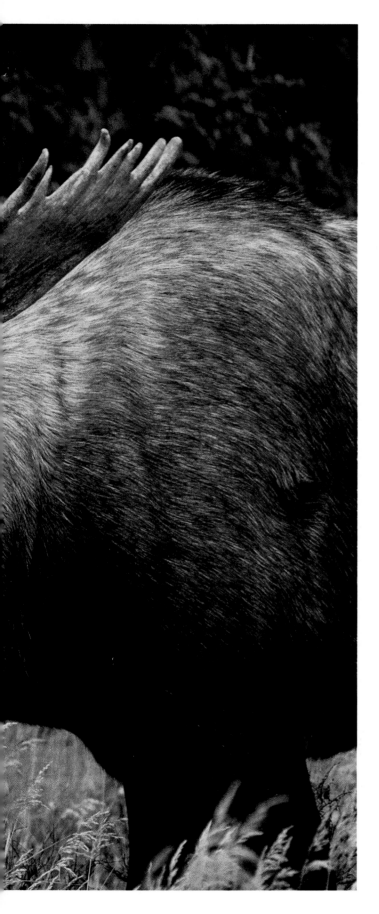

age and progresses steadily downhill from there. Moose may survive to fifteen or more years old in the wild, but their maximum longevity can't be much more, simply because their teeth are so worn down. The oldest moose on record is from New Brunswick—a cow aged twenty-two years.

Antlers

The antlers sported by an adult bull moose are its most recognizable feature. Moose antlers are unusual among the deer family in that they have broad palms connecting the tines or points. A young male calf in his first fall may develop small buttons, but they rarely protrude above the hairline and fall off in the winter. Year-old calves develop a two-tined spike or small palm. At two years of age, antlers exhibit a wider variety of patterns with multiple tines and occasionally some palmation. Three-year-old and older moose develop the classic-looking antlers that include broad palms and multiple tines.

The age of a bull moose can't be estimated accurately by the size or number of tines on the antlers, but prime older bulls—five to ten years old and in good physical condition—can produce some impressive racks. A more accurate estimator of age is the diameter of the antler near its base: the larger the diameter, the older the moose.

Antlers are bony structures comprised mostly of calcium. They begin to develop in the spring and grow rapidly through the summer, when they are covered with a blood-rich velvet. By August or September, the antlers are fully developed and the velvet falls off or is rubbed off against shrubs and trees over the course of one to two weeks. Curiously, bull moose eat the velvet they rub off, perhaps to regain precious nutrients that would otherwise be lost. The velvet-free antlers appear white at first, but continued rubbing brought on by the beginning of the breeding season stains the antlers a brown color.

Antlers are carried through the breeding season and into early winter. They are shed between November and March, the majority between December and February. The antlers rarely fall off at the same time, but may fall off within hours or days of one another. Bulls may try to rid themselves of

The skin and fur covering the growing antlers is rubbed off in late summer.

their antlers by knocking them against trees.

The timing of antler shedding varies with age. Older bulls shed their antlers early in winter and start growing new ones early the next spring. Yearlings and younger bulls may hold onto their antlers until late winter and have a delayed start to the growth of new ones. As they get older, bulls shed and start antler regrowth earlier and earlier.

Although only bull moose grow antlers as a rule, there are exceptions. In the last twenty years there have been reports of at least three cow moose bearing antlers. In each case, the antlers were small and poorly developed and still in the velvet stage. As in other members of the deer family, females occasionally grow antlers as the result of increased levels of certain hormones or injuries to a specific portion of the skull. Antlered female moose apparently retain the function of their reproductive organs as several of them have been reported with calves at their sides.

People are fascinated with moose antlers. Many folks in moose country collect them in winter and spring. Some wildlife artists use the antler palm as their canvas. The Boone and Crockett Club keeps records of trophy antlers for moose in North America. The current world-record holder is an Alaskan moose whose rack was 65 inches across weighing 55 pounds 8 ounces. The heaviest rack on record is from a moose in Alaska at 79 pounds.

Antlers provide further evidence for the separation between Eurasian and North American moose. Antlers from North American moose are larger on average. Scandinavian moose also have a much higher percentage of deerlike or "cervina" antlers, which lack well-developed palms. Additionally, in North America, the antler pattern is called "butterfly" because of the two lobes of palms on each side, which resemble a butterfly when viewed from above. In Scandinavia, bulls typically have a "shell" pattern with one large unlobed palm on each side. Alaskan moose follow the butterfly pattern, but some individuals develop a third lobe on each side. This is the pattern from the now-extinct stag moose, and some scientists have suggested that the more complex antler pattern is a characteristic that evolves in moose living in open country.

Vocalizations

Unlike many animals, moose are largely silent creatures. The sounds they produce, however, are critical in certain parts of their life cycle and under specific circumstances.

Most of the vocalizations are made during the breeding season. Bulls make a soft *"gluck"* noise, which is a nonthreatening call

OVERLEAF: Moose use vocalizations primarily during the breeding season.

Antlers harden as the velvet is shed.

Moose can see 360 degrees around them without moving their heads.

used when bulls approach each other in nonaggressive situations. Bulls that are aggressive utter a call that sounds like "*mu-wah*." Cows in heat advertising their status make a nasal melodic whine sounding like "*moo-ooo-ah*." Hunters and moose watchers often imitate this call to get a good look at a big bull.

I make this call by holding my forefinger and middle finger of both hands against the sides of my nose and forming a tent with my hands in front of my mouth. The sound comes out nasal, and I end it with a short "*uh-uh-uh*." It has worked well in Maine's Baxter State Park and on Isle Royale where bulls come hurriedly to find this "lonely cow." Those who use it successfully, swear by it. The call is sometimes made without mouth

sounds. A number 10 coffee can may be used by punching a hole in the bottom and pulling a rawhide string through the hole and knotting it on the outside. Wetting the string and pulling along it with the forefinger and thumb produces a similar sound.

Moose calves are more vocal than their parents. They bleat like a young cow or sheep when they are hungry, frightened, or separated from their mother. As they grow older, they become less vocal. Adult moose, however, will give a bleating call when they are distressed.

Moose also use some nonvocal sound signals to indicate their presence during the breeding season. Bulls like to advertise their arrival into an area by thrashing branches with their antlers and by cracking large sticks with their hooves. As with the vocalizations,

Large and movable ears give moose keen hearing.

moose can be drawn into an area by people who imitate these sounds by scraping a real moose antler, or even a plastic milk jug, against trees and brush.

The Senses

The moose is endowed with keen eyesight, hearing, and smell. Because of the position of their eyes, moose can see 360 degrees around themselves simply by moving their eyes in the sockets. To the sides, moose have monocular vision, which limits their assessment of distant objects that are not moving. They can have binocular vision, as in humans, that allows for depth perception for short distances behind and in front of them. Short-distance binocular vision is important for feeding, breeding, and when moving

rapidly through thick forests.

Hearing is one of the moose's most important senses, and large ears are immediately obvious on calves, cows, and antlerless bulls. They stand out on the calves, which are born with unusually large ears, making them look like donkeys. The ears don't grow as much as the rest of the body and seem more normal relative to overall body size on adults.

A moose's ears seem to act independently of the rest of the body, constantly swiveling from side to side and front to back like radar antenna. The moose's keen hearing can pick up a human voice a mile or more away in open country.

The moose's sense of smell is considered exceptional. The surface area of bones in their nasal cavities, on which nerve endings for smell terminate, is more than four times as large as that for a German shepherd and more than 200 times that in humans. In addition, moose have a specialized olfactory sensor called a vomeronasal organ in the mouth's upper palate. Two openings to the one-inch-long cavity lined with hairlike projections allow mucus to be pumped in and out by muscle action, which aids in the capture of airborne chemicals released during the breeding season.

Moose gesture with their bodies to give signals to other moose. Much of the signaling has to do with the social pecking order, particularly among bulls. The head and antlers are the most important parts of signals and displays between moose. Bulls of inferior rank never directly face a superior bull and move away from the superior animal without facing him. The dominant bull, however, shows his dominance by turning his head directly at the inferior bull. Large bulls of nearly equal rank display their antlers to one another to allow for an assessment of antler size. Heads are held low and antlers turned up for a good display. One bull may hold his head high and turn his antlers in a "high threat" to indicate his sense of superiority.

Cows and bulls without antlers raise up and thrash their forelegs to show aggression toward another moose. This display is sometimes used toward helicopters when biologists conducting surveys hover low to the ground near a moose.

Like other members of the deer family, a moose shows alarm by raising two patches of hair on its lower back. Alarms occur when a predator or unknown animal is sensed.

The physical and physiological characteristics of the moose have evolved over the centuries in response to a severe environment. Behavior, habitats, food habits, reproductive cycle, and mortality factors round out the ecological story of the moose.

Body language sends a variety of key messages.

CHAPTER TWO

Habits and Habitats

What defines wild moose country and how do moose use it? One part of the answer is that moose are circumpolar in their distribution, ranging across the northern forests of North America and Eurasia. Moose populations are most closely associated with boreal forests comprised of spruce, fir, aspen, balsam poplar, and birch. They also occupy eastern and western deciduous and mixed conifer forests, the transition zone between northern forests and tundra where dwarf trees are present, and aspen parklands. Their existing North American range is limited in the North by the absence of woody food plants on the treeless tundra, in the West by excessive snow depth and lack of woody plants in high-elevation mountain ranges, in the Southwest and Central Plains by temperature, water, and suitable food plants, and in the Southeast by a high incidence of a disease of the nervous system. Similar environmental factors seem to limit Eurasian populations.

Movements and Home Range

Similar to most ungulates, moose are not territorial. While they may defend an area around themselves, may drive away competitors during breeding season, and may keep other moose away from their calves, they do not maintain a specific, defended area. Instead, moose wander over an area, during the course of a year, called a home range. The home ranges of individuals overlap significantly, dependent in part on the food supply.

Prime moose habitat is the boreal forest of the northern hemisphere.

Nutritious aquatic vegetation attracts moose to lakeshores.

High-elevation meadows and forests are used by some moose in winter.

The home ranges of moose vary widely across seasons and across their global range. Some moose are seasonally migratory while others use the same area throughout the year. Extremely large home ranges exist for migratory Alaskan moose whose movements may encompass nearly 600 square miles. To the other extreme, nonmigratory bull moose in Ontario and Quebec have home ranges of only 7 to 10 square miles. In some areas, moose may range as few as 2 square miles over the course of a year.

There are consistent differences between the home ranges of male and female moose, and age also is a factor. Males have larger home ranges than females, especially during the fall breeding period. Young bulls also

wander over large areas occasionally. Bulls' home ranges vary with age while those of cows tend to stay the same.

Home ranges may vary by season. In migratory moose, that is obviously the case, but even in nonmigratory individuals there may be seasonal changes in movement patterns. For example, in adult bulls, early fall is a time of wandering in search of receptive females, and the average home range size increases. Winter typically brings deep snow (which restricts the amount of movements) and a more sedentary lifestyle. During the summer, bulls again move more widely in search of adequate food. Scientists believe that the need for bulls to maintain their larger body mass forces them to cover larger areas in search of food. During the spring, when one would surmise that cows with calves would limit their movements, they actually wander more freely than cows without calves, apparently in search of the green patches of forage they need to be able to produce milk. In a Swedish study, females with calves had home ranges in spring nearly three times larger than those without calves.

Although moose do not exhibit territorial behavior, they have a reasonably strong fidelity to home ranges occupied in previous years. Heavily hunted populations and those experiencing high predation have less fidelity than those with low mortality rates. Because most moose have traditional and predictable movement patterns, they may not recolonize vacant areas quickly even if they are nearby. Only when high densities of moose result in severe competition for food are they drawn to vacant habitat. This has been demonstrated in central Norway where a moose population has been using the same winter range at high elevations for the last 5,000 years despite a continual degradation of the winter habitat brought on by changes in food supply.

Moose seem to have limited abilities or affinities for shifting their habitat use patterns. Yet they must move out of their mother's home range eventually if they are to find enough space for themselves—unless the population is experiencing high mortality and there is no competition for food, space, and mates. Young bulls are the most likely to disperse and they seem to make the longest sojourns. When young bulls go through their first breeding season, they get the urge to seek out receptive cows. Because the older bulls dominate breeding activities, the young bulls may be forced to wander throughout the breeding season. Generally, their travels are somewhat limited and they find a suitable winter range for themselves. However, some young bulls seem afflicted with wander-

lust and undertake long-distance trips which take them hundreds of miles away from their birth area.

The habitat a moose occupies in its life may be largely dictated to it, especially if it is a cow. Female calves tend to occupy home ranges adjacent to or overlapping with their mother's. Not only do cow calves take up residence near their mother, they don't move much afterward. Thus, a cow that produces many female calves that in turn may have female calves of their own may be at the center of a loose, but complex, network of home ranges of close relatives.

This set of circumstances has the potential to create a loosely knit social organization. Nonetheless, moose are considered to be the least gregarious and social of the members of the North American deer family. In fact, they are considered solitary with only occasional groupings around scarce resources or during breeding season.

Moose Society

The solitary nature of moose is the rule everywhere except Alaska, where certain conditions have led to the evolution of social groups. We know that the ancestors of modern moose had been inhabitants of boreal forests for thousands of years. Moose that came to settle in Alaska found a different set of conditions than did those that stayed in Eurasia or colonized the boreal forests of North America. There, they found much more open habitat of tundra and dwarf willow and an abundance of large predators. Scientists believe that the combination of these two factors led to the recent evolution of group living in Alaskan moose.

Even in Alaska, moose do not congregate in large herds as do caribou and musk oxen. Their "social groups" are relatively small, consisting of two to five animals in most

Moose are solitary animals except on the Alaskan tundra where they form small social groups.

cases. However, for an animal considered solitary across its range, any group of two or more engaging in similar activity and acting in a somewhat synchronized fashion is considered social behavior.

Groups of "social" moose have been studied in Denali National Park. These Alaskan moose show several adaptations to living in a primarily open environment—distinctive markings on their pelage (the black rump patch described earlier), large body size, large and complex antlers, a haremlike mating system, and the presence of social groups. In Denali, large groups of moose are more likely to be seen farther away from protective cover than small groups. The large groups forage less efficiently than small groups or

individuals because they spend more time looking up and responding to the movements of other moose in the group.

Despite the reduced foraging efficiency, there seems to be something to be gained by moose living in groups. Moose in groups may enjoy a lower probability of predation by wolves because they are surprised less frequently. Essentially, the more eyes, ears, and noses, the better. This concept is supported by studies of predation and the reaction of moose to potential predators. The fact that cows with calves are rarely part of social groups lends further evidence. When predators pursue members of a group, they usually focus on the most vulnerable members. Cows with calves would always be most vulnerable so there is

Calves stay at the water's edge while their mothers feed.

no advantage to abandoning their solitary lifestyle, especially given the lower foraging efficiency.

The behavior these moose display is not the highly evolved social structure found in other hoofed mammals living in open environments with many predators—on the plains of Africa, for instance. There, over the course of hundreds of thousands of years, species such as zebras, antelope, and gazelles have developed a complex set of signals that warn the group of an approaching predator. Alaskan moose do not yet have these signals nor do they exhibit other facets of group living such as cooperative defense as seen in musk oxen.

Social groups of Alaskan moose are loosely organized and unstable, with lots of movement between groups. The behavior exhibited by these moose may represent an intermediate stage between solitary and group living. It seems plausible that Alaskan moose could further evolve behaviors that increase the aggressive tendencies, resulting in increased foraging efficiency and an even greater benefit to group living.

Seasonal Movements

Bulls and cows do not spread themselves over or use habitat in the same way. Studies in Denali National Park show that during the summer, cow moose adopt a strategy to protect the calves from predation by wolves and bears. They use habitats not normally used by bulls or cows without calves, namely aspen-spruce forests and birch-willow forests. Protection of the calves seems to be a stronger influence on cows than finding the best places to feed.

Bulls, on the other hand, concentrate on finding abundant, high-quality food for the summer. They use willow thickets along rivers and tall and low willow forests. Because they lose weight during the rut, large bulls need to put on all of the weight and fat reserves they can during the summer. Cows with calves are able to forage throughout the breeding season and gain weight right into the beginning of winter. The evolutionary pressure on large bulls to breed as many times as possible during the breeding season causes them to adopt a strategy of intense feeding during the summer. Bulls become much more vulnerable to predation after

the breeding season because of their weakened condition. They go into winter with lower fat reserves than cows, calves, or young bulls. Adult bulls adopt a strategy in winter of reducing predation and reducing energy expenditure in an attempt to survive the winter.

In Denali, adult bulls winter in high-elevation valleys that have willow thickets and deep snow. The deep snow, while energy-expensive for bulls, also likely limits the effectiveness of wolf predation because travel is even more difficult for the wolves. Willow thickets provide abundant food throughout the winter and the bulls don't have to forage over a large area.

Moose living at high elevations in the western United States and Canada often find snow depths that limit their movements in winter. In the Yellowstone National Park area, where snow accumulates to depths over six feet, moose face a challenge during winter. Many moose go into winter using high-elevation willow stands similar to those used by moose in Denali. As winter progresses, however, deep snow forces them to use conifer forests where snow depths are much less, but food is scarcer.

In the southern part of moose range in North America, winters tend to be less severe, but snow depths can be enough to force moose into areas with less snow. Moose "yards" during winter are less common than those of deer, which may be used traditionally over many years. Yarding behavior in moose seems to be largely involuntary and the result of limited winter cover in certain areas.

The western Upper Peninsula of Michigan is home to a new moose herd since the late 1980s. It is also in the Lake Superior snow belt, which produces some of the deepest snow in eastern North America. During early winter, moose bed in areas where the sugar maple is the dominant tree. In late winter,

Bulls often choose willow thickets for feeding and protective cover.

however, moose bed primarily in conifer forests under hemlock or balsam fir trees. Moose move from open hardwoods to increasingly heavier conifer forests as winter progresses.

The bed sites of bulls differ from those of cows with calves. Bulls tend to bed down in more open areas than those used by cows and calves. Cow beds are usually on the edges of conifer stands while calf beds are directly under the canopy of conifer trees. The inability of calves to move through deep snow may influence bed sites.

Some researchers have suggested that moose use snow in early winter as an insulated bed to protect from heat loss. Others have questioned this theory, pointing to the moose's tolerance for extremely cold conditions and relative intolerance for warmth.

Snow depth over two or three feet definitely restricts movement and habitat selection.

Calves learn about good areas for food and cover by staying with their mothers for one year.

Moose are easily heat stressed when out in the open.

Snow depth may trigger both spring and fall migration movements. For some migratory moose in central Sweden, fall migration begins when snow depths reach an average of seventeen inches and spring migration begins when snows melt to a depth of two or three inches. It appears that the ability of moose to move through the snow is not the factor that initiates the movements. Rather, the availability of food under the snow may be the important factor.

The Effects of Heat and Cold

Moose living near the southern edge of their range are subjected to greater levels of heat stress than those in the far North. The moose's large body size and effective insulation allow it to withstand extremely cold weather. These same characteristics make it highly susceptible to high temperatures commonly encountered in parts of the lower 48 United States. It is generally accepted that the southern limit of moose range is determined in large part by environmental stress brought on by heat.

To counter this problem, moose select habitats that minimize the stress from these factors. Moose often use closed-canopy forests to reduce the amount of direct sunlight on them. However, these forests may lack wind, which contributes to convective cooling. When ambient temperatures are above 60 to 70 degrees Fahrenheit, moose

may move from shaded habitats in forests to open wetlands, where they bed down in shallow water at the edge of ponds. The cooling influence of water outweighs the direct heating of the sun, and the effect of wind in open areas increases evaporative cooling. Additionally, wetland areas provide some relief from biting insects.

The large body size of bulls makes them more susceptible than cows to heat stress. Choosing high-elevation habitats under closed-canopy forests is one way they minimize this. Despite their smaller body size, cows also must deal with problems brought on by heat. Cows adjust their daily activity schedule to be most active in open areas during the cooler parts of the day. They may also be less active and move less during periods of high temperatures.

The Manchurian subspecies lives farther south than any other and endures higher summer temperatures. Its small size and thinner hair during summer are thought to be adaptations to heat stress.

Extreme cold does not seem to limit the northern range of moose. Rather, it appears to be the absence of a suitable food supply. Moose were absent from Alaska's North Slope until forty or fifty years ago, but became abundant along the Colville River until the early 1990s, when biologists noticed a sharp population decline from 1,500 to less than 400 in a five-year span. In the far North, it may be that the cold itself does not cause

moose to die, but that it stresses them, allowing other factors to come into play.

Daily Patterns

The lives of all moose revolve around finding food, and their daily activity patterns reflect this. With the exception of the breeding season, in which other interests take precedence, and the need to avoid or fend off predators, moose spend their days walking, standing, feeding, and lying. Most of the time spent lying is used for rumination of food.

Over the course of a day, moose go through a number of alternate feeding and lying periods. The number and duration vary widely by individual moose and across moose range, but there are some relatively predictable patterns.

Alaska's Kenai Peninsula moose tend to be active, that is, feeding, standing, or walking, around 60 percent of the time during daylight hours. The rest of the time is spent lying. Periods of activity are shorter than periods spent bedded down. Feeding bouts typically average just less than an hour and almost always last less than two hours, while periods of lying average about two hours and last up to four or more hours. There is no difference among bulls, cows, and calves in the duration of feeding activity. Calves, however, have lying periods averaging almost three hours, cows average two-and-a-half hours, and bulls slightly less than two hours.

There are several cycles of activity over the course of the day. Moose are typically inactive during darkness. They become active at first light, then are relatively inactive for several hours before another peak of activity. Most moose are bedded during the hottest part of the afternoon. Moose feed in the late afternoon and may feed again just before dark.

Moose can be found feeding at any time of day.

Late winter is a time of more bedding and less feeding. During the summer, moose may average around eight cycles of activity daily and spend less time bedded down. The timing of activity also varies among seasons. Because of the potential for heat stress in the summer, moose are more active during the periods around dawn and dusk and in early-morning hours when ambient temperatures are lowest. They stand or bed down in cool places during the heat of the day.

The daily and seasonal patterns of habitat use and behavior are driven by the need to find adequate food, to produce young, and to minimize the effects of predation and other mortality factors. The constant search for food is the compelling influence on a daily basis.

CHAPTER THREE

The Search for Food

Large body size and life in a cold environment place high energy demands on moose. Grown adults require forty or more pounds of food per day. This demand is satisfied with difficulty since highly nutritious and easily digestible food is available for only a few warm months each year. The remainder of the time, moose are forced to exist on a diet of abundant, but hard to digest, woody plant parts.

Techniques

Moose belong to a group of vegetarian mammals known as ruminants, species that have four-chambered stomachs and that regurgitate their food to chew it again and to recycle it through the digestive system. Their complex digestive system evolved to process large amounts of relatively undigestable plant material. The multiple-chambered stomach and an intestine full of bacteria that break down and extract nutritional value from plants are the major internal adaptations.

Externally, the moose uses its large size to reach for plant material unavailable to most other smaller herbivores. It rarely stands on its hind legs to reach high branches as deer occasionally do, but it uses its bulk to achieve the same end. A moose will readily straddle a small tree and walk over it, forcing the tree to bend over against its chest until the desirable branches are within reach. In northern Maine, along the sides of logging

A half-ton moose needs lots of calories every day.

40

Aquatic vegetation is easily digestible
and contains important nutrients.

roads in spring, I became accustomed to seeing rows of young balsam poplar trees broken off about ten feet above the ground as if they had been mowed over—evidence of the moose's strength and determination.

The moose's highly flexible and sensitive upper lip gives it dexterity to select individual plants or plant parts carefully. Browsing on twigs generally involves one of two feeding techniques. Moose often nip off the ends of branches and twigs, particularly in the winter, to get nutritious buds. During the summer, when leaves are on deciduous trees, a moose often runs the branch through its mouth, stripping off leaves, small twigs, buds, and some bark. Moose occasionally graze on low-growing plants in the summer, but it is not common. More frequently, they submerge their heads to pull up aquatic plants in shallow ponds or along lakeshores.

Browsing for Nutrition

During fall, winter, and spring, moose eat bark, twigs, and buds from a variety of woody plants. Willow, birch, and aspen, which are favorites of many other herbivores, are the most commonly eaten. As with many other plant eaters, however, moose eat a wide variety of plants. Randolph Peterson, former professor at the University of Toronto, compiled a list of fifty-seven trees and shrubs known to be eaten by moose in North America. Some of the more common species include balsam fir, striped (moose) maple, pin cherry, hazelnut, red osier dogwood, and mountain ash. Deciduous species tend to be the most important foods although moose in some populations subsist on balsam fir and other conifers. In northern Europe, Scots pine is one of the most important fall and winter foods.

It is literally impossible to describe a typical moose diet. The food habits of individual populations of moose are largely determined by availability of plants in the area. What an individual or group of moose eats is determined by the choices made in overall habitat selection and in individual trees or shrubs.

In the western United States and Alaska, moose prefer willow all year long, but may be forced into the shelter of conifer-dominated forests in winter because of deep snow. There, they browse on less desirable species such as subalpine fir, balsam fir, and other conifers including hemlock and cedar.

While aquatic plants are largely unavailable to moose in the winter, at least a few industrious moose have figured out a way to find some highly nutritious plants and the important minerals they contain. Wildlife biologists near Thunder Bay, Ontario, found moose pawing through nearly two feet of snow to eat frozen stems of horsetail. They postulated that the moose were after the sodium content, which was twenty to forty times higher in the horsetails than in other winter browse.

For many moose, their diet can be described as low quality because the most highly nutritious foods are either scarce or unavailable. For example, birches are only medium or low quality compared with other browse species used by moose. However, they are extremely common across much of moose range and they are often the most commonly eaten food just because of their abundance.

Finnish ecologists have described how moose survive on this low-quality fare. In Finland, moose browse primarily on birch. Instead of demonstrating a selective preference for certain species or sizes of twigs as they are able to do in high-quality habitat, moose use small areas for foraging. They reduce their energy expenditures by not moving around and by eating most of the available twigs on any one tree or clump of trees. This strategy leads to a higher proportion of thick stems, which are less digestible than

During winter, moose must feed on bark and twigs.

thin stems, but seems to be the one that balances energy costs of feeding with nutritional quality of available foods.

As winter wears on, many moose that started in good habitat are faced with fewer and fewer choices of food. Like moose that survive on poor nutritional food all winter long, these moose start to become less selective in their diets and often bite off larger-diameter twigs. In late winter, bark becomes a more important source of food for some moose. Moose chew the bark off aspen and red maple trees, and occasionally off balsam fir and a few other less common species. Like beavers, rabbits, and some small rodents, moose find nutrients in the layers of living tissue around the tree. Some scientists have suggested that bark eating by moose indicates a shortage of other types of food. Their use of bark primarily in late winter supports this idea, but bark is eaten at any time of year.

Many woody plants have evolved defense mechanisms against browsing in the form of secondary chemical compounds that make the plant tissues less palatable and less digestible. Many of the moose's foods contain terpenes and other chemicals known to inhibit browsing mammals like deer and hare. Some studies of moose diets support the idea that moose choose species of plants with lower chemical contents, and within a species are able to pick out individual plants with lower concentrations of the compounds.

Some moose swim into deep water and dive for food.

However, moose also seem to have a capacity for detoxifying some plants and using them for browse.

Diet Diversity

In the summer, moose continue to feed on woody browse. The greater variety of herbaceous species at this time of year, however, provides a more diverse diet. In particular, the luxuriant growth of aquatic plants attracts moose to woodland ponds and lakes where they spend a great deal of time with their heads underwater pulling up pond lilies and other plants by their roots. Feeding on submerged and floating aquatic plants is common in the East and Midwest of North America, but less so across the rest of the continent. In the drier, high-elevation part of moose country, particularly in the Rocky Mountains of Canada and Alaska, ponds and lakes are scarce and tend to support less plant life. There, moose rely on willows in riparian floodplains along river banks during the summer. For reasons not yet fully understood, moose in Scandinavia, eastern European countries, and western Russia do not feed on submergent vegetation, while moose in eastern Russia and Siberia do.

A wide variety of plant species are available in woodland ponds and lakes. Moose sample many of them, but prefer species in the genus *Potamogeton* known as pondweeds. Pond lilies, eel grass, water shield, arrowhead, bur-reed, rushes, sedges, and horsetails are eaten frequently as well.

It is a delight to watch moose feed in a pond or in the shallow bay of a large lake in summer. The best time to do so is at dawn when moose first feed for the day. In the half-light of that hour, the first evidence of a moose is usually the splashing as the animal makes its way out to chest- or shoulder-deep water. Then the head is completely submerged for thirty seconds or more and all is quiet. Suddenly, the head is brought to the surface with a great rush of water followed by the gentle sounds of teeth working over the stems and leaves of the plants. Large bulls provide the most entertainment. Their massive antlers still in velvet cause a great deal of water to be displaced when they raise and lower their heads. It is not unusual for a bull to come up with its antlers adorned with dangling shreds of pondweed.

Aquatic feeding tapers off by mid-morning and is largely absent in the middle of the day except on cloudy days. It resumes again in late afternoon and at dusk. It has been suggested that aquatic feeding is used as a way to cool off and to avoid flies. If this were the case, moose would spend far more time than they do in the water, as flies are bothersome all day long and they would cool off during the heat of the day. Just the opposite is true and it appears that feeding out in the open, even when it involves being in the water, is somewhat of a heat stress.

Use of aquatic vegetation starts around May, as soon as the ice is gone and aquatic plants have begun to grow. Maximum use occurs in June and July, and tapers off in August. Moose may still be using some aquatic plants through September and October.

Why do moose eat aquatic vegetation? Aquatic plants are more digestible than woody browse and leaves and they contain as much as ten times the amount of sodium (salt). Sodium is a mineral often in short supply for herbivores and they often feed deliberately on plants with high sodium content. There has been a controversy over the primary reason for eating aquatic vegetation. Just how important is the sodium?

Plant-eaters must maintain a specific ratio between sodium and other minerals in the body, particularly potassium. Potassium levels are high in early summer in many of the terrestrial plants eaten by moose, while the sodium levels in those plants remain unchanged. To compensate for this and to maintain a favorable sodium-potassium balance, moose may seek out plants with high levels of sodium, such as emergent and submergent aquatic plants. The levels of potassium in terrestrial vegetation drop to normal levels for the rest of the year.

The sodium hypothesis may partially explain why moose in Europe do not feed on submergent vegetation. There, the sodium content of woody plants is two to ten times higher than in the equivalent browse in North America. Therefore, they may not need aquatic plants to meet their sodium requirements. However, when they occasionally feed on emergent aquatic plants such as horsetail, they select the species with the highest sodium content. Researchers are puzzled why moose in this area wouldn't use the underwater plants with an even higher sodium content.

Another hypothesis offered for explaining moose use of aquatic vegetation is based on the ideas that aquatic plants grow in greater densities than terrestrial plants and can be foraged on more efficiently, they are more digestible, and they occur in a habitat in which moose are invulnerable to predation and therefore can reduce the amount of time they have to be vigilant for predators while feeding. It seems likely that aquatic foraging by moose is governed by several factors that differ in importance across their range.

OVERLEAF: Moose feed in ponds during the summer and early fall.

45

Leaves and twigs comprise some of the summer diet.

Plant Communities

Moose can have a tremendous impact on the plants they eat. Individual species respond differently to having their leaves, bark, buds, and small branches chewed off, but many of the primary foods of moose are plants that have evolved to deal with moderate amounts of browsing.

Collectively, moose can have a large effect on the composition of entire plant communities through their browsing activity. They can alter the abundance of species, change the growth form of the plants, and affect the system in which energy and nutrients flow through the soil and living organisms. In turn, the effects moose have on plants can influence

the trends seen in moose populations. The spectacular fluctuations in numbers of moose on Isle Royale have been driven in part by changes in plant communities brought on by the browsing done by moose.

In Denali National Park, Alaska, researchers found a complex web of relationships between moose, the plants they browse on, and the soil supporting the plant community. Moose were attracted to high densities of willow and browsed them extensively. The browsed plants produced leaves that were more easily decomposed by microorganisms living in the soil. Urine and feces deposited by moose in the areas where they fed approached the level of commercial fertilizer and the plants responded with increased

growth. Similarly, the soil microorganisms flourished and nutrient turnover in the soil was high. Essentially, the activities of moose created a positive feedback loop through fertilization and browsing.

In an area near Fairbanks, researchers from the University of Alaska found that leaves from birch trees browsed by moose decomposed faster in streams. Because streams receive most of their energy input from leaves as opposed to plants growing in the stream, the decomposition rate of leaves in streams affects the growth of aquatic insects and the fish that feed on them. Their study supports the idea that terrestrial and aquatic ecosystems can be tightly linked and that the moose can be a keystone species that

determines many features of plant and animal communities.

On Isle Royale, the effect of moose browsing on trees has been studied for several decades. Small fenced areas that prevent moose from browsing inside the areas provide a stark contrast to places where moose browse regularly. Most of Isle Royale is a boreal forest dominated by aspen, birch, spruce, and fir trees. Aspen and birch are the pioneer species after disturbances such as fires or the workings of beaver. Over time, the conifer trees slowly replace the aspen and birch if there is no disturbance event.

Moose prefer aspen and birch for food and secondarily browse on balsam fir. Over much of the island, moose have been so plentiful and

disturbances so infrequent that aspen and birch occur in relatively small numbers. Balsam fir has become the primary food for moose on the island. Most balsam fir seedlings never get a chance to grow higher than a few feet tall because of constant and heavy browsing by moose. The result has been a steady increase in the amount and dominance of spruce trees and an overall change in the composition of the forests on the island. Moose do not like to eat spruce because of its low amounts of nutrients and high amounts of resins. Balsam fir has declined severely in its abundance on the island since the arrival of moose around 1900. Before that time, fir trees comprised approximately 46 percent of the forest cover. By 1978, fir accounted for only 13 percent and today comprises about 5 percent.

Inside the browsing exclosures, a much different forest exists. There, the balsam fir seedlings grow unfettered by browsing pressure and develop into mature trees. Dominance by spruce trees is not so evident.

Researchers on Isle Royale have also linked wolf predation on moose as a factor that affects the composition and growth of trees on the island. A study of tree rings showed that periods of better growth as indicated by wider tree rings occurred only when wolf populations were at high levels and moose were at low levels. Thus, high rates of wolf predation effectively released trees from moose herbivory for a few years until the moose population recovered. This has happened in a cyclic pattern for decades and will likely continue as long as there are wolves and moose on Isle Royale.

Fire plays a significant role in the food habits of moose. While catastrophic wild fires can temporarily destroy a food source, the result of fire is the release of nutrients tied up

Moose calves learn what to eat by watching their mothers.

in trees and other vegetation. Pioneer species respond positively to fire and these are the plants preferred by moose.

Fires have been suppressed by government agencies in the last hundred years and prescribed fire is a largely unused tool. Commercial timber harvesting has replaced wild fire as the dominant disturbance factor in boreal forests. Fortunately for moose, logging often produces the same result for desirable moose foods and moose readily use cutover areas.

The search for food is a dominant activity for most of the year. However, the need to find food to stay alive and healthy is not an end unto itself. For a moose, food keeps it in a holding pattern to ensure that it will be in prime condition for the breeding season.

A moose's diet and metabolism change in the fall.

CHAPTER FOUR

The Reproductive Cycle

The urge to pass copies of genetic material from one generation to the next is strong in the moose. This evolutionary pressure influences much about the moose's physical and social characteristics. For moose, almost everything revolves around the short, fall breeding season. Then males and females, which have been living separately during the rest of the year, come together for just a few brief days to carry out the rituals passed down through the generations for thousands of years and to create new life for the following spring.

Reproductive Biology

Male and female moose go through annual cycles of physical and physiological changes starting and ending at different times, but both peaking during the fall breeding season. The cycle for a female starts in late summer when her body undergoes internal changes associated with the development of eggs and the preparation of reproductive organs for breeding and conception.

Most kinds of deer—including moose—have several egg production cycles, which gives them multiple opportunities to be bred successfully. Cow moose come into heat during the second ovulation cycle. It is unknown why there is no breeding behavior during the first egg cycle. A cow stays in heat for a day or two and will allow a bull to breed her at this time. If there is no breeding, a cow cycles through heat again about twenty-five days later. Although it rarely happens in wild populations of moose, cows can cycle through heat six or seven

The urge to create new life brings cows and bulls together during the short mating season.

Newborn calves carry the genes of future moose generations.

A bull tends a cow in heat before mating.

times during a breeding season, which would extend into March. Typically, however, cows are impregnated in the fall, conceive and carry young for about 230 days through the winter and into spring, give birth, and raise young through the summer into late summer when the cycle renews itself.

For bulls, the reproductive cycle starts in the spring when antlers first begin to grow. Like the peacock's feathers, antlers are an adornment related almost exclusively to breeding, and the bulls have no use for them once breeding has ended. Bulls have increased levels of testosterone in their bodies in summer; this causes the antlers to harden and leads to increased production of sperm cells for the upcoming breeding season.

The period of active breeding for moose is called the rut, a time when bulls and cows seek each other out, engage in breeding behavior, and eventually mate. The moose rut begins in early fall, as much as two months earlier than the late fall deer rut. The rut can last for as little as a month. After this period, the testosterone levels in bulls drop dramatically, leading to an eventual shedding of the antlers in early winter for older bulls. Males are reproductively inactive through the winter until the cycle is renewed in the spring.

Unlike white-tailed and mule deer, male and female moose do not become reproductively active until they are sixteen months old. If they are in poor physical condition, they may not gain reproductive status until they

Chemicals in a cow's urine indicate her readiness to breed.

are twenty-eight months old. Biologists often use pregnancy rates of yearling cows to determine the condition of a moose population. The higher the percentage of sixteen-month-old cows that breed, the better overall condition of the population. While young bulls may be physically capable of breeding after their first full year, they rarely get an opportunity to do so because older bulls dominate them behaviorally and do most of the breeding themselves.

In a typical moose population, most of the animals are calves and juveniles. Young bulls do very little breeding, while all of the young cows typically breed. The most productive cows are those four to twelve years old, while bulls five to ten years old do most

of the breeding. Cows thirteen years and older and bulls older than eleven years continue to breed, but their smaller numbers and decreased status means they contribute very little to future populations.

Breeding Behavior

The environment in which moose have evolved has shaped their breeding habits. The overriding factor seems to be the timing of birth in the spring. Moose occupy highly seasonal environments and the probability of calf survival is limited to a relatively narrow window in the spring. Those born too late in the spring are at a distinct disadvantage, as they are unable to put on enough weight to

Ritualistic sparring determines which bulls will be dominant and breed.

get them through the winter. Thus, there is a strong urge in moose to complete breeding early and over a very short time period.

Other factors influence the breeding pattern as well. Because moose live at low densities in boreal forests and the sexes are separated throughout the year, they have had to develop behaviors that are effective ways of getting together during the short period in which females are in heat. In addition, cows must have ways to assess the fitness of bulls to be sure that the sire of their newborn calves has good genes.

Moose have evolved two distinct breeding strategies, each designed in response to their basic environment. Over much of Alaska and the Yukon Territory, where moose occupy open tundra habitat, moose often breed in groups similar to harems of species like elk. Over the rest of moose range, where they occupy forested habitat, moose breed in pairs.

Moose do not form true harems, but bulls establish large breeding areas and advertise their availability to cows by leaving urine scent marks. Cows move into the area before they come into heat and stay until they are ready to breed. Unlike true harem breeders, bulls do not tend the cows to keep them in the group. The dominant bull may have to defend his female group from other large and small bulls that roam the periphery of the group challenging the dominant bull and attempting to court and breed cows while the dominant bull is busy. The size of a moose harem can be from just a few cows to as many as a dozen and varies over time as cows move in and out of the group.

In forested areas, bulls do more searching for cows. As each cow comes into heat, she advertises her upcoming readiness to breed by urinating and calling using a low moan. Bulls use these auditory and olfactory signals and even call back to find cows in thick forests. Once a bull finds a cow, he stays with her for up to several days until she is bred.

Several males may be attracted to the same female and ritualized fighting may occur to determine which gets to breed her. While antlers are formidable weapons, the evolution of large antlers is primarily for display. Antler size is an indication of

Bulls scrape shrubs to make noise and indicate their presence to other bulls.

male quality and cow moose can quickly assess their best mating partner in part by the size of the rack. Bulls also can quickly judge the value of getting into a fight in which one or both might be injured or even killed. Assessing antler size is done both visually and by sound.

During the breeding season, bulls scrape and rub trees and shrubs with their antlers. The sound of a large antler with big palms is very hollow, and carries for miles. Their acute hearing allows bulls to size up potential rivals and their locations just by listening closely. Smaller bulls are dominated by bulls with larger racks by just seeing them. An older bull with a rack size more equal to that of a dominant bull may need to be chased away repeatedly before he accepts the larger bull as dominant. Only when two bulls both think they have the larger rack does serious sparring usually occur. Sparring is dangerous for

both participants. Puncture wounds are common. Occasionally, antlers become locked and the bulls are unable to break free from one another.

During the rut, mature bull moose stop feeding altogether for a period lasting two or more weeks while they concentrate solely on breeding cows. Their weight decreases significantly and they become vulnerable to predation in late winter if they are unable to regain the weight. Younger bulls do not cease feeding totally and cows do not change their feeding behavior.

This puts mature bulls at a distinct disadvantage, and they try to breed as many cows as they can during the fasting period. They use several ways to attract females and to induce the cows to come into heat to maximize their breeding output for the year.

At the beginning of the rut, mature bulls paw out a small depression in the ground about three or four feet in diameter and urinate in it. Their urine at this time of year has a strong, musky odor reflecting physiological changes important for the breeding season. They splash the urine on themselves and wallow in the pit to spread the odor over their bodies. Younger bulls typically don't dig pits.

Cows and small bulls are very interested in the pits dug by the old bulls. Both attempt to wallow in the pits to spread the urine-soaked mud all over themselves. The old bulls try to keep the younger bulls out of the pits. While any cow is usually provided access to the pits, the cows may fight among themselves to determine which gets to use the pit first. Cows also rub their bodies against those of mature bulls that have been wallowing in an attempt to get the mud and scent on themselves. In areas where group breeding occurs, the most impressive breeding ritual revolves around the pit. A bull wallowing in a fresh pit attracts the cows in his group, which move slowly around him in a circle, in

what some biologists have called a "dance," like odalisques in a harem.

While scientists have not been able to experimentally demonstrate that the chemicals in the urine of bull moose cause cow moose to come into estrus, the evidence supports such a contention. Several independent studies have shown that the majority of breeding occurs over a one- or two-week period and that up to 80 or 90 percent of the cows are bred at that time.

Why younger bulls try to get the urine-mud mixture on their bodies is a bit of mystery, but it appears that they try to attract females to rub against them so that they can start to form a bond and have a chance at breeding them when they come into heat. Cows sniff the bodies of the bulls before they approach them, perhaps in an attempt to determine their breeding status. The younger bulls lose nothing if the cows reject them since they have little chance of breeding success. Some, however, are able to fool a cow now and again.

Bulls also produce chemicals in their saliva during the rut, which may be important in priming the cows for breeding. The saliva drips onto the chin and into the bell below the chin where it is smeared onto cows in a behavior known as chinning. When the cow rubs her body against the male to get urine and mud on herself, she may also rub underneath the bull's chin, presumably to get some of the saliva compound.

Unlike the females of most species of hoofed mammals, cow moose actively search out males because the probability of a mature bull finding her during the short breeding period is low. One way cows advertise their presence and readiness to breed is the marking of small trees. Typically, they find a small, pole-sized tree and strip the bark and branches off it three to four feet above the ground. The bark is not eaten. Then, they rub their

Cows mark trees with their scent.

head, neck, and ears on the stripped area, leaving scent from glands in this region of their body.

Cows mark trees early in the breeding season. Bulls engage in the same behavior, but don't do so until late in the rut. It is likely that only cows that missed breeding during their first or second estrus cycle are attracted to the sign posts, which may serve to prime them for another heat period.

Cows and bulls show interest in marked trees and there appears to be some relationship to dominance, since cows or bulls dominant over the individuals that made the initial marks may leave their own scent on top of the other.

All of the effort moose go through to make themselves attractive to one another, to ward off competitors, and to find one another during a short breeding period is culminated with an even shorter set of actual

breeding activities. A cow about to come into heat is tended by a bull in either a harem or singly. He periodically approaches her slowly with an outstretched neck, flicking his tongue, and giving a low croaking sound. The bull smells her genital area, particularly after she urinates.

Like other hoofed mammals, bull moose have a stereotypic behavior, called lipcurl or flehmen, which occurs after smelling a cow moose's urine. The lipcurl directs odors to the mouth and nose where an organ allows males to assess the breeding readiness of a cow. When she is receptive to mounting, she allows the bull to place his chin on her rump while she slowly walks. If the mounting sequence is unsuccessful, she may come back and smell the bull's nose and rub her head against his sides and rump.

Copulation is decidedly brief, lasting all of five seconds. Typically, one copulation is all that occurs in females in harem groups. A single cow being tended by one bull, as is the case over most of moose range, may be bred by the same bull more than once during her heat. Unlike elk and some other members of the deer family, moose do not have noticeable post-copulatory behavior. They tend to drift back to their normal pattern within minutes of completion of breeding.

The majority of bulls in a moose population do not breed. Large, dominant bulls do most of the breeding and some of them may breed ten to twenty cows during the rut. The competition for females ensures that the calves to be born in the spring have genes from the biggest and strongest males.

The New Generation

While prime bulls, exhausted and weight-depleted from the rut, go off to find good winter food sources, cows carrying the spark

Calves are nearly always born in dense vegetation.

of new life start an approximately eight-month pregnancy, which they must maintain through a long winter. Most cows of breeding age have become pregnant in the fall, typically 80 percent or more.

If yearling cows were in good physical condition, most of them were bred. In a population of moose in good nutritional condition, females in the prime years of their lives—between five and eleven years old—have a good chance of carrying twin calves through their pregnancy. The proportion of cows with twins is often related to the density of moose in an area. When a moose population has nearly reached the limit of the habitat to support it, twinning rates may be less than 5 percent. In a growing population, however, in which food is not limiting, as many as 90 percent of cows older than two years may give birth to twins.

Moose calves have large ears and short snouts.

Moose calves weigh 30 pounds at birth and can stand and walk within 2 days.

Triplets are not out of the question—I saw a cow with three very young calves on the shores of Grand Lake Sebeois in northern Maine in the early 1980s—but are the clear exception. The champion moose cow seems to be a Minnesota moose living in the Horseshoe Lake Area of the Boundary Waters Canoe Area. In 1992 she apparently birthed and raised four calves.

The outcome of pregnancy is largely dependent on the condition of the cow before she was bred and the amount of food she is able to find and consume during the winter. Experiments conducted on captive moose have shown that cows eating as much as they wanted gained weight throughout the winter and gave birth to healthy calves during the normal calving period. On 85 percent of those rations, cows lost weight and gave birth a little later, but the calves were comparable in size to those born in the other group. Cows fed only 70 percent rations lost considerable weight, gave birth almost a month later than normal, and despite the calves weighing about the same as those in the other groups at birth, most of them died within a day of birth. Thus, the length of the pregnancy is dependent in part on the development of the calves, and calves are not born until they are fully developed even if it means as much as a month longer pregnancy. Cows in an extremely poor nutritional situation either abort the fetuses spontaneously, produce still-born young, or if early enough in the pregnancy, may reabsorb the fetus.

Most cows in a region give birth in a very narrow two-week window of time. In far northern latitudes, this is between the last week of May and the first week of June. In the southern part of moose range, the calving period is during the second and third weeks of May.

The evolutionary factors that have influenced the timing of calving in moose are not known. They may include the concept of predator saturation. This occurs when animals whose newborns are very susceptible to predators, but become less so within a few weeks of birth, all give birth in a short time period and literally overwhelm the predators with too many choices. Each cow's calves then have a greater probability of escaping predation during their most vulnerable period.

Predation on newborn calves appears to be the factor influencing the selection of calving sites. Across moose range, most cows choose calving sites where either their chances of encountering predators are low, where there is thick hiding cover, where they can detect predators easily, or where there is an escape area or refuge nearby. In some areas, calving sites do not seem to have any special characteristic other than being good moose habitat.

The choice of islands or peninsulas as

Cows give birth to just one calf when moose densities are high.

calving sites is perhaps best documented. Their likelihood of being confronted by a bear or wolf is extremely low at these sites.

Typically, cows separate themselves from the calves born to them the prior year before moving to a calving site. They may arrive at a calving site a few days to a few hours before giving birth. At some island sites, there is evidence that cows advertise their presence to other cows looking for good areas to calve by scraping a small depression in the ground and perhaps urinating in it.

Moose calves are relatively helpless at birth, but can stand and walk within a day or two. Some calves swim before they are a week old. The protective nature of mother moose is well known. Cows with calves occa-sionally charge humans and their natural predators and may aggressively chase off a bull that gets too close.

Calves typically weigh 25 to 35 pounds at birth. Single calves are usually heavier than twins. Moose calves are the fastest-growing land mammals in North America, putting on two to three pounds per day and weighing 300 pounds by fall. Calves rely on their mother's milk exclusively for the first month and are gradually weaned from nursing by around four months. Their intake rate peaks at about three weeks old when they consume thirteen pounds of milk per day. Moose milk is higher in protein and fat than cow or goat milk.

Calves stay with their mothers through their first summer, fall, and winter. When she

Moose calves gain weight rapidly and can weigh 300 pounds by fall.

is ready to calve again, she separates herself from the yearling, although the young moose is reluctant to break the bond that has been strong for an entire year. Occasionally, the yearling is allowed to accompany the new family group for a time after calving.

Calves learn a great deal about their home range by spending the first year with the cow. The association between the cow and calf is so close that they are rarely separated by more than a few yards. When cows forage on underwater plants, their calves often stand up to their bellies in the water. The close association also provides an opportunity for calves to learn about food and they may feed on species of plants similar to those on which their mothers feed.

The survival of moose calves depends on many factors, including the experience of the mother. Because many of today's moose populations exist in areas where wolf and bear predation is not high, a large percentage of calves survive through their first summer and fall. Their first winter may prove to be the most difficult period. In moose populations where predation is a significant factor, 40 to 50 percent survival through the first summer and fall is typical.

The addition of calves is what keeps a moose population going. At the same time, the size and density of the population and the available food resource limits how many moose calves will make it to adulthood. Overlaying everything are the vagaries of Nature, from extremely harsh winters to wild fires that renew depleted range. The common thread running through all circumstances is the endless attempt for each moose to pass on some of its genes into the future.

CHAPTER FIVE

The Seamless Fabric
of Life and Death

The moose's struggle to survive is played out on a stage with other characters that rely on the moose for their own source of nourishment and ultimate survival. From man and other large predators to tiny microorganisms, the intersections of life and death become blurry the closer we look.

Moose have coexisted with predators for their entire existence. Their large size has made them less vulnerable to medium-sized predators and has reduced the numbers and kinds of predators they must face. Today, only very large predators or those that hunt in groups pose a threat to moose.

Moose also suffer the effects of a wide range of parasites and diseases. While the brainworm has garnered the most attention, other factors affect individual moose, and some sweep across entire populations.

Predation by Bears

Most parts of wild moose country are also inhabited by black and brown (grizzly) bears. Bears are omnivores, feeding on both animal and vegetable materials, and are largely opportunistic predators.

When bears emerge from their winter dens in spring, they have used up most of their fat reserves and are in need of protein and energy. Available protein in plant material is limited at this time of year because plants have just started to grow. Both species of bears satisfy some of their nutritional needs by preying on newly born deer, moose, and elk.

Bear attacks are one of many mortality factors moose face.

A bull moose holding his ground is a formidable opponent to most predators.

Moose calves are unable to defend themselves and are not proficient at eluding predators during the first month or two of life. Bear predation on moose calves occurs primarily in the calves' first thirty days of life. After that time, calves are capable of outrunning a pursuing bear and predation rates from bears drop.

Moose calves represent a highly digestible source of protein to bears. This may be especially important to female bears that have borne cubs in the den and continue to have high energy requirements associated with nursing them. A moose calf provides about a week's worth of energy requirements for an adult female black bear, making it highly worthwhile for a bear to search out moose calves. On Alaska's Kenai Peninsula, researchers have determined that the vigor of the black bear population, especially cub survival and growth, is influenced by the moose numbers in the area and that nutrition gained from preying on moose calves in spring is the key. Adult black bears rarely prey on adult moose or yearlings unless they are weakened by disease or other factors such as old age or an injury.

Brown bears also focus on moose calves, although their size, strength, and speed make them more capable of dispatching an adult moose. Much of the research on brown bear predation has occurred in Alaska where they are still abundant. In one study in south-central Alaska, researchers radio-collared 198 newly born moose calves. Brown bears were the primary mortality factor, killing 87 calves (44 percent) in the first six months.

Brown bears may actively seek out moose calves in spring to satisfy the same nutritional needs as black bears. While brown bears don't actively hunt for adult moose, they take advantage of opportunities presented to them and will attempt to kill a moose taken by surprise or an adult moose made vulnerable by

other factors. Adult cows with calves tend to be most vulnerable, but bulls in rut or immediately following rut and any malnourished moose in spring are prime candidates for brown bear predation. Brown bears often chase a moose to water where they are able to more easily dispatch it without being injured.

Both black and brown bears are fond of carrion and may scavenge moose carcasses left over from winter kills by wolves. Bears are always interested in a meal of fresh meat and will approach a wolf pack feeding on a freshly killed moose. In general, wolves fend off black bears in these interactions, but often defer to brown bears.

The effects of bear predation on moose populations varies by its intensity and other factors. In general, it is not thought to be a significant factor limiting or regulating moose populations. In places like Alaska where there may be predation by wolves, brown and black bears, and humans on the same moose population, bear predation may be significant in combination with the other mortality factors.

In parts of Russia where brown bears are still relatively abundant, predation from bears exerts a stronger influence than in many other parts of moose range in Eurasia. The effects of brown bear predation decrease from north to south with 4 to 5 percent of the moose population killed annually by bears in the north, 2 to 3 percent killed annually in the central part of Russian moose range, and 1 percent of moose killed in southern areas. Pregnant cows and calves are most susceptible.

Of Moose and Wolves

The gray wolf is the most significant and effective predator of moose in North America and northern parts of Asia. In fact, wolves evolved their social behavior and hunting style primarily in response to the

The wolf is the primary predator of moose over most of its range.

need to dispatch moose and other large hoofed mammals, most of which dramatically outsize them.

Wolves live and hunt in cooperative social groups called packs. The success of the pack depends on the cohesiveness of the unit and the collective contributions of each member. This is especially true when they are hunting large, dangerous prey like moose.

Because moose tend to be solitary, with the exception of cow-calf associations, wolves must seek out individual animals. Once they detect a moose, they must determine if they have a good chance of killing it. This process often involves the testing of an individual moose to see if it shows signs of vulnerability. In other cases, wolves quickly assess that a moose is far too strong and healthy and don't waste their time in what would be a fruitless effort.

Assessment of a moose's vulnerability is important to wolves for two reasons. First, they can't afford to use up energy when there is little hope of regaining some of it through a kill. Second, moose are extremely dangerous to wolves. The front and hind hooves are used as effective weapons by moose, and many wolves are killed or seriously injured with a kick to the head or body.

Moose and other potential prey of wolves avoid predation in several ways. Selecting habitats little used by wolves reduces their detection. Once detected, moose and deer choose different strategies.

Antlers and sharp hooves are used in defense.

Unlike white-tailed deer, which defend themselves from predators by running and showing their white tail flag, moose that successfully resist wolf predation do so by standing their ground.

Each encounter between wolves and moose is different and the success of the attempt by wolves depends on a combination of factors including the age, sex, condition, and experience of the moose; the size, composition, and experience of the wolf pack; the season of the year; the environmental conditions; and perhaps more. Therefore, it is difficult to describe a "typical" encounter between moose and wolves. In general, however, the deciding factor is whether or not the moose flees when it is initially encountered. If

it does not flee, the moose rarely loses. If it runs, it signals to the wolves that it may be vulnerable and its chances of surviving the encounter go down markedly. Over the years, scientists have discovered that wolves catch and kill fewer than 8 percent of the moose they encounter and chase.

Some researchers have been fortunate enough to witness encounters between moose and wolves and have provided descriptions of successful and unsuccessful predation attempts. One encounter in which the wolves were successful occurred in winter and involved a pack consisting of the adult male and female and their three pups of the year, which were not yet experienced hunters. This wolf pack detected a solitary cow moose that began to run when it sensed the wolves near-by. The wolves gave chase and the adult male wolf, called the alpha male, started biting the cow's hindquarters. The alpha female did the same on the other leg. The moose kicked out repeatedly and the wolves dodged the blows. Finally, the alpha male darted in and bit the left haunch and held on. The moose began to kick furiously and continued to run with the wolf holding on. The alpha female acquired a similar hold on the other leg and the moose dragged both. The wolf pups, although near-ly as large as their parents, were excited and followed the moose, but did not move in to attack the moose on other parts of the body as more experienced pack members would have done.

The adult wolves each weighed over 75 pounds, but the moose was strong enough to drag both of them. She ran through the forest causing the wolves to be bounced and rubbed against trees and downed logs. Despite the punishment they received, the wolves held on and the moose began to tire. The cow even-tually weakened from loss of blood and from the expended effort, and came to a stop. The wolves released their grips and remained close while the cow stood feebly by. The pups stayed back at the edge of the small clearing they were in until the moose collapsed in the snow. Finally, all of the wolves moved in to start feeding.

Each successful predation attempt by wolves is different, but their strategy is clear-ly to attack the hindquarters and to inflict enough injury to cause excessive bleeding so that the moose eventually becomes weak enough to approach safely. Moose have learned this strategy and attempt to guard their hind legs. Some moose back up against a tree or a small group of bushes to keep the wolves at bay. Cow moose help defend their calves by taking a position at the rear of the calf and protecting the calf's hindquarters from bites by wolves.

Obviously, the more wolves in a pack and the more pack members that are experienced hunters the more the scales tip toward the wolves. Similarly, the older, larger, healthier, and more experienced the moose, the greater the chance it will be able to successfully defend itself.

In general, bull moose in their prime are the least vulnerable to wolf predation. Newly born calves tend to be the most vulnerable. Adult cows without calves and young bulls in good condition are less vulnerable than old moose of either sex and than older calves.

Wolves are expert at assessing the vulner-ability of moose. When researchers have an opportunity to examine the skeletal remains of a wolf-killed moose, they often find broken bones, deformities, impacted teeth, or some other factor that affected the moose's physi-cal condition.

One of the more interesting recorded wolf-moose interactions involved an old bull moose spotted almost a mile away from Isle Royale on Lake Superior ice. Researcher Rolf Peterson reported how tracks in the snow told the story of repeated attempts by wolves to attack the moose, which held its ground and kept the wolves at bay. Flying over the moose in a small airplane, the researchers noticed that the moose responded to the sound, but not the sight of the plane. They landed and determined that the bull was blind or nearly so in both eyes. They contin-ued to check on the moose for several days. It moved farther out on the ice and eventually died, although not from the wolves, which had given up the effort. Even with its sight disability, the bull had somehow amazingly fended off the wolf pack at least two times in open ground.

Age, sex, and physical condition are not the only factors affecting the vulnerability of a moose to predation. Snow depth and the

Heavy snows can give moose an advantage over their shorter-legged predators.

type of snow can have a great effect on both moose and wolves. Snow can act as an ally or foe to moose and can change as fast as the weather. In general, deep snows favor moose because they are able to move around in it with their long legs far better than wolves. However, when deep snow becomes crusted and can support the weight of a wolf, the balance tips in the wolves' favor. Snow rarely becomes so heavily crusted that a moose can be supported. For that reason, during winter, wolves often hunt for moose along shorelines of lakes and try to induce moose to leave the protective cover of the forest, with deep snow that likely is not crusted, for the frozen lake, which may have had the snow blown off it or have crusted snow. Experienced moose do not panic and stay in deep snow.

Wolf predation on moose also varies by season, and reflects the relative vulnerability of age-sex groups at different times of year.

Typically, calves are the primary prey in late spring, summer, and fall. Adult cows and bulls are killed in summer and fall, but in low numbers. Adult cows are killed most frequently in early and mid-winter. Adult bulls become vulnerable in late winter and early spring due to depletion of energy reserves.

There is some evidence to suggest that the patterns of snow depth on a year-to-year basis may also affect moose vulnerability to predation. What some researchers have come to believe based on wolf predation on different age classes of moose is that consecutive years of deep snow limits moose movement and the ability of cows to forage effectively. These cows are in worse physical condition than during a normal winter and they bear young that are less fit. After several years of deep snow, calves born to cows surviving the winter are in extremely poor condition. Some of these calves are not killed by wolves and become young adults, which typically are not particularly vulnerable to wolf predation. However, because they were born malnourished, they do not escape the vulnerability factor, and continue to suffer high mortality from wolves. Young adult cows born as malnourished calves may give birth to calves that are themselves extremely vulnerable. So, condition may not be determined by the food a calf eats after birth, but by the condition of its mother in prior winters. Thus, its vulnerability to wolf predation may have been set in motion by the snowfall of previous winters.

Wolf-killed moose provide food not only for wolves, which may feed on the carcass for a week. Scavengers such as red fox, coyotes, weasels, wolverines, fishers, gray jays, blue jays, chickadees, magpies, and ravens all benefit from the death of an individual moose. Bald eagles may find late-winter food uncovered by melting snow in the remains of a moose. The circle of life revolves endlessly

Snow can affect the physical condition of cows and their calves.

through living and dead moose and the creatures that carry some of the moose in them through their own life cycles.

The Moose of Isle Royale

Isle Royale National Park in western Lake Superior is home to the most studied herd of moose in the world. Moose either swam or crossed on the ice from the Canadian mainland fifteen miles away around 1900. Wolves were not present until the late 1940s when they crossed on the ice one winter. By then, the original moose colonizers, which had expanded to 1,000 to 3,000 animals by the late 1920s, had already experienced cyclic booms and busts from overuse of the food supply.

The moose population on the island has continued to fluctuate in a cyclic manner over the years. The wolf population has done the same. Wolf numbers are not tied to the numbers of moose. Rather, they reach highest levels when the numbers of moose nine years old and older are high. At this age, moose become very susceptible to wolf predation.

In the late 1980s, wolf numbers on Isle Royale declined sharply and biologists feared they would become extinct on the island. It wasn't until the early 1990s that wolf numbers began to rise again. Meanwhile, the moose population was crashing from an all-time high of approximately 2,400 in 1995 to only 500 in 1997. The seemingly healthy moose population was affected by low survival of calves, retarded body growth of calves from a declining food source, a deep-snow winter, and a high incidence of winter ticks. Together, these factors produced the highest mortality rate of moose in almost forty years. Nearly 80 percent of the moose died in just one winter.

Recent poor calf production and survival

Antlers provide a source of calcium for forest rodents.

and a moose population skewed toward older-age animals will cause the moose decline to continue for a few more years until food supplies are more favorable. At 2,400 animals, moose had reached the limit of their food supply on Isle Royale and had nowhere to go but down. The population density at that time of 13 per square mile was the highest in the world.

Other Predators

While wolves and bears are the primary predators of moose throughout their range, other predators can be effective in certain locations under specific conditions. Mountain lions are the only other North American predator large enough to regularly kill moose. The Rocky Mountains of western Canada and the northwestern United States are one of the few places where the ranges of

One moose can supply a wolf pack with several weeks of food.

Calves are more vulnerable to predation than adults.

moose and mountain lions overlap.

Despite their size, mountain lions are more apt to wait in ambush for an elk, white-tailed deer, or mule deer. In parts of the Rocky Mountains in southwestern Alberta, however, female mountain lions prey on mule deer and elk, but male lions focus on moose. In one study, the diet of male lions was 92 percent moose. Calves and yearlings were killed most often. Unlike wolves, mountain lions stalk their prey and then launch a sudden rush. Caught by surprise, a mother moose may be scared off and the calf killed quickly while she is gone.

The Manchurian moose, which lives in northeastern China, southeastern Siberia, and Mongolia, is the only subspecies of moose preyed upon by tigers. Although very rare at present, the Siberian tiger shares a few places with moose and is a regular moose predator.

Mid-size predators, such as coyotes, may prey on moose calves occasionally, but moose are not the likely focus of their hunting activities as is the case for wolves. One of the more unusual accounts of predation on moose comes from Alaska where two moose swimming across an ocean inlet were attacked by a pod of killer whales. Only a rare set of circumstances brings these two species together.

The Brainworm Connection

Predation by wolves and other mammals

Brainworm can debilitate the healthiest of moose.

is not generally considered to be a limiting factor for moose or a cause of moose population declines, although it may keep moose numbers low in certain areas under specific conditions. For the last thirty years, moose biologists have attributed moose population declines and limited range expansion to the south on the small internal parasite, *Parelaphostrongylus tenuis*, known as brainworm.

Throughout the twentieth century, biologists have been aware of a condition they termed "moose sickness," which causes moose to exhibit abnormal behavior including repetitive circling, loss of the fear of humans, and aimless wandering. Other symptoms include partial paralysis of the hindquarters and partial blindness. In all cases of moose sickness, the animal eventually dies.

The cause of moose sickness was unknown until the 1960s when it was definitively proven that a small internal parasitic nematode was the cause of the disease. This meningeal flatworm is extremely common in white-tailed deer where it lives in the layers of tissue surrounding the brain and the spine. Infected deer show no outward signs of problems and the parasites are considered relatively benign. In moose, elk, and caribou, however, infections are fatal. In moose, the parasites live in the eyes and central nervous system.

P. tenuis has a complex life cycle that relies on at least two animals and specific conditions. During one stage of its life cycle,

Unhealthy moose may produce small antlers.

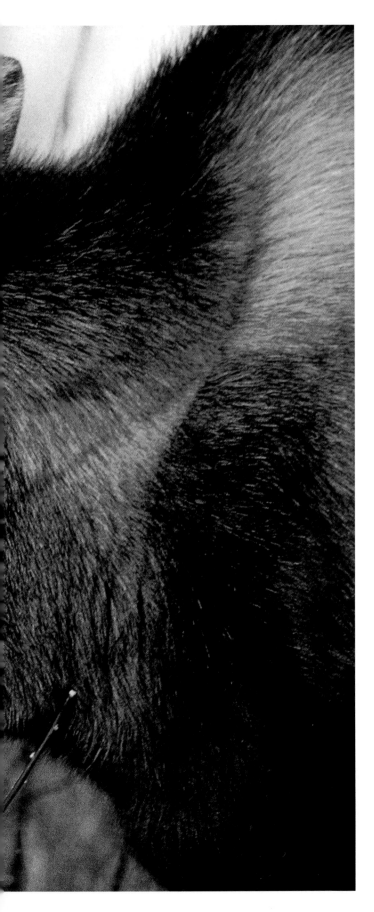

its larvae live in the tissues of ground-dwelling snails and slugs common in forested regions of eastern North America. These species are occasionally eaten incidentally by white-tailed deer during grazing. The larvae leave the snail's or slug's body in the deer's stomach and penetrate the stomach wall. They move through the body cavity to the spinal cord where they mature into subadults. Subadult worms migrate to the head and occupy spaces around the brain and spinal cord and in the sinuses where they become adults. Eggs laid by the adults hatch into first-stage larva, which migrate to the circulatory system and are eventually carried to the lungs where they erupt in the lung tissue, are carried up the respiratory tract, are swallowed by the deer, pass through the digestive system unharmed, and are passed out of the body with the feces. Snails and slugs feeding on fecal material become infected and the cycle is complete.

In moose, the activities of the nematode can cause lesions in the brain and on the spinal cord. Eggs are sometimes laid in the brain and in the eye, causing blindness. Unlike deer, moose sometimes show outward physical signs of the infection, including abnormal antler structure if the worms invade the part of the brain where the control of antler development occurs. Because the disease brought on by the infection was considered fatal, the life cycle was never considered complete when a moose was the host. The fatal nature of the infection also prompted biologists to believe that moose sickness could be the cause of some population declines of moose and the factor limiting moose from expanding into areas with high populations of white-tailed deer. They also used it to explain how moose survive in areas where white-tailed deer are abundant, invoking a "refuge" explanation.

These ideas changed with the successful reintroduction of moose to Michigan and the natural recolonization into the New England states. In those areas, moose have been successful despite the presence of deer, and despite individuals becoming infected and showing signs of moose disease. Now, it has become evident that the relationship between deer populations, the brainworm, and moose populations is more complex than originally thought.

Biting flies and external parasites plague moose.

Moose population declines are often associated with deer densities of 14 per square mile or greater, but there are numerous examples of places where moose have persisted at low numbers despite high numbers of deer and a high incidence of brainworm in deer feces. The documented persistence of moose in areas where infected deer are present suggests that the effect of brainworm on moose populations is more subtle than has been believed.

In 1982 a wildlife scientist in Nova Scotia reported the completion of the life cycle of the brainworm in moose. This suggested that the disease may not always be fatal and that moose and the nematode may be co-evolving toward a more tolerant relationship. Researchers from Maine discovered first-stage brainworm larvae in 10 percent of moose pellets in part of Baxter State Park in the late 1980s, further supporting the idea that moose can harbor brainworm without fatal results.

Moose biologists now believe that moose do not have to occupy refuges where deer densities are low in order to survive in areas with overall high deer densities. In fact, moose populations may be able to expand even when there are cases of fatal brainworm infections because the rate of transmission between deer and moose may be low. Lastly, individual moose may survive infection and become a more important host for the brainworm as they are able to tolerate its effects.

Biting Flies

Most of us never get close enough to a wild moose to see the vast swarms of flies that hover around the head and rump. I once passed through a huge cloud of flies trying desperately to keep up with a swimming moose and was nearly blinded and choked by them.

Mosquitoes, black flies, no-see-ums, deer flies, horse flies, and other well-known biting flies of northern forests all feed on moose blood. One fly, aptly named the moose fly, is specific to moose. Large horse flies may be called moose flies in some areas, but the scientifically recognized moose fly is a smaller fly that gathers in swarms around moose.

Moose flies rely on moose blood for food and lay their eggs in moose feces. They typically appear on moose in late May or early June and stay active on moose until late September. Moose flies are short-lived, perhaps only thirty days, so there may be two or three generations on an individual moose over the course of the summer. The flies gather around the head, rump, and backs of the hind legs where they feed on blood and tissue fluids from open sores. The combination of types of biting flies can produce open lesions on the hindquarters that do not close and start to heal until the end of fly season in the fall.

Any parasites or diseases that affect hair can cause problems in winter.

As many as 500 moose flies may be on an individual moose at one time. Both sexes of fly are present and they feed in small groups, typically around the edge of open sores. Female moose flies deposit their eggs in fresh feces within thirty seconds of defecation and then return to the moose.

Bothersome flies cause moose to flick their ears, shake their heads, stomp their feet, and shake their entire body. Moose have been observed lying down in mud, which may relieve the biting around legs. However, unlike caribou and other members of the deer family that may seek windy ridges to reduce the stress from biting flies, moose seem to tolerate them without changing their overall activity pattern.

The advent of fall and cold temperatures of winter would seem to be a relief for moose that have had swarms of flies around them since spring. For many moose, however, an equally bothersome and potentially more damaging insect pest becomes active in winter.

External Parasites

Although a number of external parasites have been found on moose, the winter tick, *Dermacentor albipictus*, is the only one considered to be of importance. The winter tick is a blood-sucking parasite that overwinters on moose, deer, and other wild ungulates in southern Canada and the northern United States. The moose is its primary host. It is

Dozens of internal parasites can affect moose in apparently good condition.

found on many moose during the winter, and an individual moose can have as many as 100,000 ticks on it. When ticks occur in large numbers on moose, they can cause anemia, depletion of fat reserves, and premature loss of winter hair. During some years, many moose are found dead with large numbers of ticks attached. In Minnesota, winter ticks are commonly found on moose, particularly in the northwestern part of the state. Hunting seasons have been adjusted periodically when tick infestations have caused death or poor condition for moose in localized areas.

Winter is generally a time of energy conservation for moose, and they spend more time lying down and engage in fewer energy-expensive activities. Infestations of ticks often cause moose to groom repeatedly by rubbing against trees, shaking, and scratching with their hooves. The result is an increased use of energy stores and some hair loss. Researchers in Ontario documented slower weight gains of captive moose calves infested with winter ticks and suggested that the condition of calves infested with ticks may affect their survival during winter.

Internal Parasites

Numerous species of internal parasites afflict moose. In his classic midcentury treatise on moose, Ontario biologist, Randolph Peterson, listed twenty-three including tapeworms, flukes, nematodes, whipworms, bladderworms, nodular worms, bot flies, and lungworms. They were found in a variety of organs including the eye, stomach, lungs, liver, heart, intestines, nose, and skeletal muscles.

Most internal parasites do not affect moose so greatly as to cause widespread death, but there are records of individual and small numbers of moose dying as an apparent result of unusually high loads of parasites. Rumen flukes, which inhabit the rumen chamber of the moose's four-chambered stomach, are one of the parasites occasionally blamed for poor health or death of individual moose. Rumen flukes are picked up during the summer when moose feed in aquatic environments. The flukes attach to the walls of the rumen and can cause loss of the fingerlike projections important to digestive capability.

Nature recycles every part of a moose.

Diseases and Contaminants

There have been few studies of moose diseases unrelated to internal or external parasites. Periodically, scientists identify the cause of death for a moose exhibiting unusual behavior as a disease that had not yet been recorded for moose. These include pneumonia and brucellosis. Unidentified viral diseases are suspected for some moose that exhibit particular symptoms.

Scientists have reported the presence of heavy metals in the tissues of moose. The greatest concern seems to be with cadmium and copper, which accumulate in the skeletal muscles and liver. Studies have been conducted to determine if the concentrations of these elements are high enough to pose a human health hazard from consumption of moose meat. To date, there is no evidence to suggest that hunters and their families should avoid eating moose flesh. However, there is a high enough concentration in some

individual moose to warrant further monitoring and research.

In early 1996, a Swedish scientist reported that more than 1,500 moose have died in southwestern Sweden near Gothenburg since the mid-1980s from a toxic imbalance in concentrations of copper and molybdenum in their livers. The moose appear to waste away and are listless, fearless of humans, and have difficulty walking. The area is one of the most acidified in Sweden. Many of its lakes, agricultural fields, pastures, and forests have been treated with large amounts of lime for over a decade in an attempt to counter the effects of sulfur dioxide air pollution. An unwanted result of liming has been the increased availability of molybdenum to plant-eaters like moose. Excessive amounts of molybdenum can lead to a copper deficiency and death. Despite strong recommendations for action from some sectors of the scientific

OVERLEAF: In Alaska, brown and black bears are important predators of moose.

85

Moose occasionally die from drowning.

Other Mortality Factors

In the absence of large predators, moose die primarily from diseases, hunting, starvation, old age, and accidents. The increase in numbers and expansion of moose into areas of human habitation has dramatically increased the number of moose-vehicle accidents. Other accidents are a far less significant mortality factor.

The most commonly reported accidental cause of death is of moose falling through ice and drowning. While moose are excellent swimmers, they occasionally fall through thin ice and are unable to get back up on the surrounding thicker ice. Water deaths of this type are common enough in Alaska, northeastern Siberia, and parts of Canada that wildlife officials receive reports about them annually. Calves attempting to follow their mothers across large bays in spring and summer occasionally drown when they are overcome by large waves.

Moose occasionally die from becoming mired in deep bogs. Large peatlands are common in much of moose country, but this form of mortality is no doubt largely unrecorded by people because of the vastness of bogs and the infrequency of human visitation to them. In Nova Scotia, a moose hunter discovered two bogs in the Cape Breton Highlands with dozens of moose bones along the edge. The bog mats surrounding the small open water areas prevented moose from exiting after they went into the water to feed and created a natural trap for unwitting animals.

Although moose don't frequent the same kind of country as bighorn sheep and mountain goats, they live in rugged enough terrain to occasionally have accidents from falling down steep slopes. Others fall into pits such as old mine shafts. On Isle Royale, in the winter

community, the Swedish government is proceeding very cautiously with studies to determine how widespread this effect may be.

In the Ukraine, the fallout of radiation from the accident at the Chernobyl nuclear facility in 1986 continues to pose health hazards for people and wildlife. A large amount of radiation was released in prime moose habitat. Now, as people and moose repopulate the area and people begin to use moose as food, officials are concerned that people will unwittingly expose themselves to high concentrations of radiation in moose meat.

An unusual disease of moose is now being reported with alarming frequency in the southern region of Norway. There, numerous moose are being found with broken legs that can be attributed to osteoporosis, a weakening of the bones. No cause for the problem has been found to date.

Deep snows can cause moose to forage in steep, dangerous areas.

of 1996, almost a hundred moose fell to their death off steep, ice-covered shoreline ridges. The moose were in these dangerous areas looking for food because deep snows prevented them from feeding in inland areas.

There have been infrequent reports of moose dying or becoming badly burned from forest fires. A more frequent incidence is of adult bull moose dying from fighting during the breeding season. Sometimes, two bulls engaged in a sparring match get their antlers locked and are unable to extricate themselves.

Moose on Isle Royale often die from old age, a phenomenon not common across moose country. Because the moose population has been so well studied there, researchers have been able to document some of the conditions afflicting moose in old age. Examination of skeletal remains indicates that osteoarthritis, osteoporosis, advanced tooth wear, and periodontal disease affect successful foraging and evasion of predators.

Despite the numerous threats from predation, parasites, disease, contaminants, and accidents, moose populations are capable of thriving across most of wild moose country. For thousands of years moose have demonstrated a seemingly remarkable ability to withstand all that Nature has to offer.

CHAPTER SIX

Origins and History

The moose belongs to a group of hoofed mammals called ungulates and to a subgroup of hoofed mammals with an even number of toes called artiodactyls. It is the largest living member of the deer family, Cervidae, which also includes caribou, elk, and deer. The name "moose" is derived from a Natik Indian word, *moos,* itself descended from a Proto-Algonquian Indian word, *mooswa,* meaning "animal that strips bark off trees." Moose go by different names all over the world. In North America, they are moose, but in English-speaking countries of Europe, they are known as elk. In Denmark, they are *elg;* in Sweden, *alg;* in Finland, *hirvi;* in Germany, *elch;* in Russia, *los;* and in France, *orignal.*

Moose all over the world, although commonly referred to as elk in Europe and Asia, are classified as the same species, *Alces alces.* They are the only remaining species in the genus *Alces,* which finds its closest living relatives in the deer family. At one time, Eurasian moose were thought to be a different species of moose than those in North America. Despite two recognizable forms—the European–West Siberian moose, which has small antlers, and the American–East Siberian moose, which has antlers twice as large—current taxonomical thinking places all moose in the same species, but differentiates among nine geographically distinct subspecies or races.

Four subspecies occur in Eurasia and four in North America. A ninth subspecies, the Caucasus moose (*Alces alces causcasicus*), which occupied parts of southeastern Europe in Russia, disappeared in the early nineteenth century, probably from over-exploitation by humans.

Moose all over the world belong to one species.

The moose is called "elk" in Eurasia, which causes confusion among visitors from North America.

Antler shape and size vary among subspecies.

Eurasian Subspecies

The four remaining Eurasian subspecies were thought to be three until 1982 when Russian taxonomists classified a new subspecies. The race inhabiting all of northern Russia was called the Siberian elk (*Alces alces pfizenmayeri*). The Russian scientists split this subspecies in two and called the very large moose occupying eastern Siberia *Alces alces buturlini*. The newest subspecies is thought to be the closest relative to the ancestor of modern moose.

During the comings and goings of glacial sheets that advanced and retreated over much of the northern hemisphere, Siberian elk appear to have colonized new areas

whose populations, after millennia of isolation, evolved into separate races. Three relatively small races came into being in Eurasia. In southern Europe, the extinct Caucasus moose appeared. In Scandinavia, western Europe, and western Russia, a relatively small form known as the European elk (*Alces alces alces*) now exists.

Siberian elk colonizing southeastern Siberia, northern China, and northeastern Mongolia evolved into a small race of moose called the Manchurian elk (*Alces alces cameloides*). Adult bulls of this subspecies rarely weigh more than 700 pounds. The Manchurian elk also has antlers with longer tines and smaller palms than other moose subspecies. The small body size may have

Today's moose evolved from a small deer of the open plains.

resulted from poor nutrition in its glacial refugium and the more deerlike antlers are thought to be the result of genetic changes brought on by nutritional stress.

In Europe, the presence of a large ice sheet over much of Scandinavia during the last glacial period forced moose to move to central Europe. The retreat of those glaciers proceeded at an uneven pace with the warm Gulf Stream to the west allowing melting to occur more rapidly there than to the east. As a result, current moose populations in Norway and Sweden appear to be the descendants of recolonization efforts from both directions. Differences in the shape of antlers of moose in the two areas further supports this idea. Moose populations in central

Europe and the eastern part of Russia apparently underwent dramatic population cycles over tens of thousands of years. Most recently, as in North America, moose expanded to the south into countries like Poland.

Today's moose are descendants of a line of large deerlike creatures that roamed the northern regions of the planet during the Ice Age. Scientists can trace the heritage back to a time between 2.5 and 1.8 million years ago to an area in what is now southern France. At that time, the climate became cool and dry and the cool, dense forests of Europe were replaced by parklike savannahs and open grasslands with few trees. As the forests opened, deerlike animals evolved into larger forms and antlers took on a more significant role in visual communication.

The earliest known member of the moose family was known as the Gallic moose. It was a small moose by today's standards, barely as large as a yearling American elk. Scientists believe it was a speedy runner that evolved on the open plains. Its antlers were different from those of today's moose with very long beams and tiny palmate branches at the ends.

Eventually, moose and other members of the deer family evolved large forms. These relative giants spread northward and eastward and started to occupy habitats that had been vacated by forest-dwelling ungulates. They moved quickly to the northeast into Siberia as the glaciers advanced more quickly in Europe than in Asia. There, they ran out of space since the Bering land bridge had not yet been exposed. Eventually, they were able to spread into North America.

In Eurasia, an extremely large form of moose called the broad-fronted elk evolved and spread across the continent. It weighed twice as much as the largest moose alive today and had antlers that spread ten feet and probably weighed over a hundred pounds. It crossed the Bering land bridge about a half million years ago, well before modern-day moose, and occupied much of North America up until 10,000 years ago. Also known as the stag-moose and given the scientific name *Cervalces*, this species resembled the moose in most ways, but had unusual antlers with a large plate growing out of the bottom of the antler down toward the ground. *Cervalces* fossils have been found in a wide band of states across the middle of America, suggesting that the species survived until after the disappearance of the Wisconsin ice sheet 8,000 to 10,000 years ago.

This large form of moose became extinct after the Ice Age along with most other Pleistocene megafauna, such as giant beaver, saber-toothed cats, woolly mammoths, and giant bears. Large animals such as the stag-moose undoubtedly attracted the attention of aboriginal humans, who also colonized North America over the Bering land bridge. Now-extinct forms of moose were hunted by humans for food, clothes, and tools. Although the theory is unproven, anthropologists suggest that a combination of climate change and intense hunting pressure by humans caused the rapid decline of large North American species, which had not been previously subjected to such effective predation.

Humans and moose coexisted for centuries in Europe and Asia. In the late Pleistocene Era, after the retreat of glaciers, moose ranged all over northern and central Europe and northern Asia. The fossil record and historical accounts indicate that moose were found as far south as Romania, northern Italy, and the Pyrenees Mountains. During the time of the Roman Empire, moose were abundant in the Black Forest of Germany. Paintings of moose in caves date back to the sixth and ninth centuries in Eurasia and some paintings depict moose in domestic situations. Undoubtedly used primarily for food, Eurasian moose were nonetheless domesticated in some areas. This apparently occurred thousands of years ago, and in the Middle Ages, moose were used as draft, pack, and riding animals. They carried up to 275 pounds on their backs and pulled sleds loaded up to a ton. Moose were even hitched to sleds and used like horses to ferry human passengers around.

Although recent studies have indicated that moose can also be used as dairy animals, there is no evidence that they were used as such in Europe, unlike the caribou (reindeer), which was domesticated and is still used as a dairy animal in northern Scandinavia. Early settlers to Canada domesticated moose in some areas, but domestic moose today are limited to research institutions. Extensive

Wild moose have been captured and domesticated in Russia.

All North American moose have palmated antlers.

studies of moose domestication were carried out in Russia during the twentieth century. While no mass domestication program has been initiated, moose showed great promise as meat, milk, and draft animals. Three moose farms still exist in Russia where domestic moose are used for meat and milk production.

North American Subspecies

Ancestral forms of moose first appeared in North America between 250,000 and 100,000 years ago. They, along with many other mammals, crossed the Bering land bridge, which connected Asia and Alaska when sea levels dropped during glaciation. While the evidence clearly suggests that modern-day moose evolved in Asia and

dispersed into North America, it is not clear how the four separate races evolved.

It is quite possible that the first subspecies to appear was the Alaskan moose (*Alces alces gigas*), which is the largest race of modern moose. Arriving around 10,000 years ago, it may have further colonized North America during retreats of the glaciers or, as some researchers have suggested, may have dispersed into areas south of the glaciers following a glacier-free corridor through western Canada. On the other hand, there also is evidence to suggest that the first subspecies were those that eventually split into the three most southern subspecies and that the Alaskan moose appeared only 10,000 to 14,000 years ago and was limited by glaciers to only a small area in Alaska.

Recent genetic studies suggest that the first hypothesis is true. If so, all of the divergence into subspecies occurred rapidly, based on adaptations to different habitats after glaciation.

If the second—and more traditional—view is true, the story of moose evolution in North America may go something like this: During the most recent period when the glaciers advanced farthest to the south, there were four separate refugia in North America in which scientists believe moose existed. Although surprising to many people, there was a large unglaciated area in central Alaska where the Alaskan moose probably survived and remained isolated from other subspecies. Its large body size was no doubt an adaptation to the extremely cold conditions there. The other three refugia were in the Rocky Mountains of the American West, an area south of the Great Lakes, and an area in the southern Appalachian Mountains. These refugia were effectively isolated from one another by the ice to the north, extensive grasslands to the east and west, and inhospitable climate and habitat to the south. In each of the three refugia, a new subspecies evolved.

In the Rocky Mountain refugium, a medium-sized moose now referred to as the

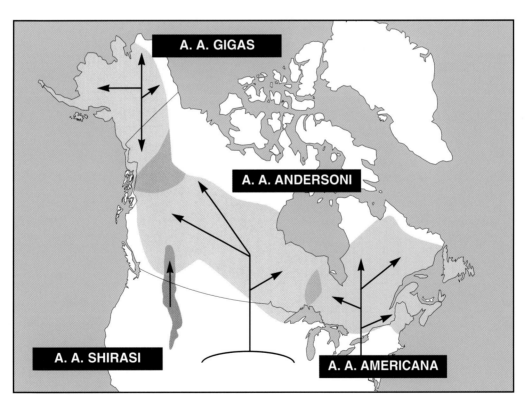

Dispersal of the different subspecies of moose in North America as the glaciers receded.

A. A. GIGAS   A. A. AMERICANA

A. A. ANDERSONI   A. A. SHIRASI

Moose continue to evolve in response to climate and other forces of Nature.

Yellowstone moose (*Alces alces shirasi*) evolved. It now occupies Idaho, Montana, Utah, Colorado, Wyoming, and southern parts of British Columbia and Alberta. The Northwestern moose (*Alces alces andersoni*), also medium-sized, found sanctuary south of the Great Lakes, then followed the glacial retreat north into Minnesota, Wisconsin, Michigan, western Ontario, and west and north into British Columbia, Alberta, Manitoba, Saskatchewan, and the Yukon and Northwest Territories. The Eastern moose (*Alces alces americana*), another medium-sized variety, moved northeast and north from its southern Appalachian refugium into New England, the Maritime provinces, Quebec, and eastern Ontario.

The glacial retreat took thousands of years and moose responded to the changes in plant communities that occurred over time. In general, they started to inhabit areas after the first woody plants, such as willow and aspen, colonized them. Eventually, the four distinct subspecies came together and occupied a fairly contiguous range across the continent. There is evidence to suggest that moose were still responding to climatic and vegetation changes when the first European settlers arrived in North America.

For example, the Northwestern moose living in the refugium in the upper Mississippi River valley south of the Great Lakes were forced to colonize new forests to the north as their path to the east was blocked by lakes, and to the west by the enormous Lake Agassiz in present-day Minnesota. The forests developing to the south were not favorable to moose and were colonized by white-tailed deer. Moose had to spread north through a narrow strip of land between Lake Superior and Lake Agassiz. The boreal forest they depended on was limited to some degree by the glacial rocks of the Canadian Shield from which much of the soil had been scraped by the glaciers and by Hudson Bay and its surrounding swamplands. When the ice dam holding back the waters of Lake Agassiz broke and the water drained away, it left fertile soils on which the forest recolonized quickly, and moose spread into that area.

While all this was happening in midcontinent, moose occupying the refugium to the east were crossing the St. Lawrence River and expanding north and east. This expansion happened slowly and scientists believe that the eastern and midwestern moose populations had not yet met north of Lake Superior as few as a hundred years ago. The postglacial expansion of moose had not reached Cape Henrietta on the shore of Hudson Bay in the mid-1900s, but in the last fifty years moose have appeared there. Similarly, it has taken time for moose from the eastern refugium to populate parts of eastern Canada. Moose were still moving into Labrador thirty years ago and have not yet fully colonized that province. Their current movement into Labrador is being hastened by roads and human settlements, which generally create younger forests more favorable to moose.

The same pattern of colonization appears in the Northwest. Recent evidence suggests that the Northwestern moose has been slowly moving northwesterly into areas previously unoccupied by moose or formerly occupied by the Alaskan moose. In British Columbia's Wells Gray Provincial Park, about 250 miles northeast of Vancouver, moose are only recent inhabitants to the Clearwater Valley. When the area was first visited in 1877, explorers found no moose, nor were they in other parts of central British Columbia. Moose first appeared in 1923 and an extensive fire in 1926 changed older forests to young ones within which moose prospered.

Over the last several hundred years, Alaskan moose have been moving into previously unoccupied parts of Alaska. All of the recent movements by moose, however, have been influenced by human changes to moose habitat and to moose numbers.

The Decline of the North American Moose

By the time European explorers were making regular trips to North America in the middle 1500s, North American moose populations had colonized much of the area formerly covered by glaciers and were probably abundant throughout their range. The first known recorded account of moose by a European came from Samuel Champlain, a French explorer. In 1603, he described an animal quite similar to the European elk which he referred to as *orignac*. A written account by an English explorer named

Young moose and some subspecies grow small antlers without palms.

Morton in 1632 describes how early explorers viewed the moose:

"First, therefore I will speak of the Elke, which the Savages call a Mose: it is a very large Deare, with a very faire head, and a broad palme, like the palme of a fallow Deares horne, but much bigger, and is 6 footewide between the tipps, which grow curbing downwards: he is of the bignesse of a great horse."

Moose were undoubtedly a preferred source of food for European settlers. Their large body size made them a desirable prize. As exploration continued, and settlement pushed westward from New England and eastern Canada into the St. Lawrence River Valley and the area around the Great Lakes, moose were hunted more intensively and over a large area. Detailed accounts written by Jesuit missionaries indicated that moose were an important source of food and clothing

The abundant moose populations were dramatically reduced during the settlement of North America.

for Indians and food for missionaries, explorers, and settlers.

The arrival of settlers changed the way Native Americans viewed and used moose. Before European settlement, moose were used for clothing, tools, and food. Trade was limited to minimal bartering among tribes. The advent of settlement created a market for moose meat and Native Americans hunted moose more intensively and used moose meat and hides as trade items for materials they had no other way of procuring—kettles, fabrics, guns, and other manufactured goods.

There is no way of accurately estimating the populations of moose nor the harvest. Anecdotal evidence, however, suggests that it was locally high in some areas. The famous French explorers, Radisson and Groseillers, claimed to have killed 600 moose near Lake Superior in one spring around 1660. Records from individual traders or trading companies list hundreds of moose skins per year over several years.

By the early 1700s, written records began to report a decline in moose numbers and in some areas, dramatic decreases or virtual extirpation. This pattern continued throughout the 1700s and into the early 1800s in many settled areas. Writers of the time and biologists since then have attributed this primarily to overexploitation by human hunters. While it is quite likely that heavy hunting pressure played a role in the decline, there may have been more to it. It appears that forest fires and changes in the social fabric of the continent played an equally major role in causing a decrease in moose populations over a large area.

The early wave of settlement in the late 1700s and early 1800s was followed by several other waves of human activity that affected moose. The logging eras across New England, Canada, the Lakes States, and into the Pacific Northwest brought many hungry people who relied in large part on wild animals for food. Railroad construction, military activities, and the clearing of land for agriculture all brought renewed pressure on moose and other wild game used for food. Only with game laws and the increased reliance on domestic animals for meat in

Heavy hunting led to the disappearance of moose in many areas.

the late 1800s did moose populations begin to rebound.

The pattern was repeated in state after state and province after province. In New York, the once abundant moose was extinct by the early 1860s. In Massachusetts, they were gone several decades earlier. Vermont protected what few moose remained in the state with the passage of game protection laws in 1876. Montana's moose population was nearly gone until the establishment of Yellowstone National Park in 1872. The early 1800s were difficult for moose in New Brunswick, where a law preserving moose in the province was enacted in 1786 but permitted to lapse in 1792. Heavy hunting pressure and perhaps other factors kept numbers low through most of the nineteenth century.

In Nova Scotia, a law closing the moose hunting season for three years starting in 1874, and another law prohibiting hunting moose with dogs and snaring probably prevented extirpation in the province.

In wilder areas, moose found refuge and probably were able to maintain reasonable numbers through the 1800s. These populations served as reservoirs allowing natural recolonization of areas in which their numbers had been reduced or eliminated. The early 1900s found moose populations on the rebound across much of their range. The passage of game laws and the practice of scientific wildlife management enhanced their recovery.

Moose found refuge from people in wild places.

CHAPTER SEVEN

Return of the Native

The settlement of North America brought three new forces to bear on the continent's moose population. Subsistence and market hunting created a new level of mortality, which lowered population numbers as hunters, trappers, and settlers moved into the Northwoods. The first wave of human explorers was followed by the great logging era, which changed the age and composition of the northern forests. Subsequent raging wild fires and attempts at farming converted prime moose habitat into unsuitable lands. Finally, populations of white-tailed deer exploded in the southern parts of Canada and in the northern United States, resulting in high levels of brainworm, which effectively limited moose wherever high deer densities occurred. By the end of the nineteenth century, moose populations in the southern parts of their North American range had severely declined.

In Russia, Scandinavia, and eastern Europe, moose numbers have fluctuated dramatically over the last 200 years. From 1700 to 1850, moose numbers were at an all-time low. Moose disappeared from vast areas and survived in only isolated sanctuaries away from human persecution. From 1850 to the 1900s, the moose population of western Eurasia expanded, only to dip again and reach a low ebb between 1915 and 1925. Starting in 1945, the numbers of moose have increased and the range has expanded. Information about moose in eastern Asia is sketchy and no clear picture of historic population patterns can be determined.

Successful reproduction is key to continued moose recovery.

Moose populations began to rebound in the middle of the twentieth century.

Moose were protected from hunting in many areas where populations were low.

The end of the twentieth century has seen a resurgence in moose populations across the southern edge of their range. From Canadian refugia and strongholds, the moose has repopulated New England states and parts of the Midwest and Northwest on its own. Purposeful transplant programs in Newfoundland, Colorado, and Michigan have accelerated what might have happened naturally. Refuges in Siberia and far northern Scandinavia held moose that have recently repopulated southern Scandinavia, Russia, eastern Europe, and central Asia.

Status of Moose Populations in the Mid-1900s

In 1937, the United States Fish and Wildlife Service began compiling estimates from states with moose populations to get an approximate size of the overall population. While the estimates from the states were not derived as scientifically then as they are today, they give an idea of how low moose numbers remained through that period. In the first year, 1937, there were an estimated 13,346 moose in the United States (excluding Alaska, which didn't become a state until 1959). Numbers fluctuated for the next ten years between a high of 17,900 in 1947 and a low of 11,584 in 1940. As the century reached its halfway point in 1948, the estimate was 11,700.

The status in individual states at that time lends perspective to where the moose population stands going into the end of the century. In the Pacific Northwest and Rocky Mountains, moose were present only in Montana, Idaho, and Wyoming. Oregon considered moose to be present only as stragglers in the Blue Mountains in the eastern part of the state, despite a small reintroduction effort that brought five Alaskan moose to the state in 1923. The last survivor from that effort was believed to have been killed in 1931. In Utah, occasional sightings in the Wasatch and Uinta Mountains were considered "accidental." Washington State reported rare stragglers likely from British Columbia in the 1940s, but considered moose otherwise absent. Colorado was considered too far south for moose, but they were recorded to occasionally stray into the state.

In Wyoming, the explorations of George Shiras in Yellowstone National Park from 1908 to 1910 discovered a fairly large herd of moose, which later came to be known as its own subspecies and which was named in honor of Shiras. This population grew steadily with the protection afforded by Park status since 1872. The State Game Warden's annual report in 1908 indicated a change from a "handful of moose" around 1900 to a "respectable number of animals" in 1908. The annual report in 1912, the year the State Legislature opened a hunting season on moose, cited 500. By 1948, the statewide population was estimated at 3,200.

In Montana, adjacent Yellowstone National Park also served as a source for repopulating the state. Surveys conducted by Vernon Bailey in 1918 found a few moose in Glacier National Park in the northwestern part of the state, suggesting that some repopulation occurred from British Columbia wanderers. In 1945, Montana declared an open hunting season on moose, with a limited license system. Montana's 1948 estimated herd was 3,100.

As with Montana and Wyoming, Idaho benefited from the protection afforded moose in Yellowstone National Park. By 1948, their population estimate was 1,000, although it had been twice that just two years earlier. The hunting season, closed since 1898, was reopened in 1946.

In the Lakes States, only Minnesota and Michigan harbored enough moose to consider them permanent residents. In Wisconsin, moose had apparently been quite abundant during the time of early exploration in the late 1600s, but by the 1900s their numbers were reduced to occasional stragglers from Minnesota in the northwestern part of the state. The last reported animal before midcentury was an ear-tagged straggler from Michigan's Upper Peninsula. North Dakota's moose population was probably never large in recent times and may have been confined to the Turtle Mountains and to forested areas in the Red River Valley. The moose's status in 1948 was as an occasional straggler into the Turtle Mountains.

Minnesota started protecting moose from hunting in 1922, but state officials felt in 1945 that the statewide moose population had increased little since that time. Some gains had been made in selected areas, such as the Red Lake Game Refuge in northwestern Minnesota where habitat improvement work

Canada's moose served as sources of moose recovery in North America.

had been attempted. Moose remained present across the entire northern tier of counties in midcentury, but were largely absent from the rest of the state. The overall population in 1948 was estimated at 1,100 animals.

Michigan had lost its moose from all but Isle Royale by the early 1900s. State officials released 69 moose from Isle Royale into the Upper Peninsula between 1935 and 1937. Poaching and brainworm were thought to have prevented this small herd from firmly establishing itself. Not many were considered present in 1948, when the statewide population including Isle Royale was estimated at 775.

The Northeast's moose population at midcentury was confined largely to Maine. New York had no moose despite a reintroduction effort into the Adirondack Mountains in 1904. Pennsylvania and Connecticut considered themselves south of

Alaska's vast moose population has remained large.

moose range despite some evidence to suggest that moose had occurred there at one time and occasional sightings in the early 1900s. Massachusetts reported only occasional wanderers in the 1940s and Vermont estimated only 10 moose statewide despite protection by law since 1876. In New Hampshire, only the northern reaches of the state were thought to hold a permanent population numbering around 50 in 1948, although hunting had been outlawed since 1901. Maine's once abundant population stood at an estimated 2,500 animals in 1948 despite complete protection since 1935 when the last hunting season had occurred.

Alaska's moose population remained largely unknown despite numerous references to their distribution in the early 1900s. The vastness of the state and its relative wildness prevented accurate estimates. Moose populations were not reduced as they were in the lower 48 United States. In fact, during the early part of the century, they began appearing in parts of Alaska where they had never been seen before. In the late 1940s, the best estimate of Alaska's moose population was 30,000 to 60,000 animals.

Canada was and is the heart of moose range in North America. Like Alaska, much of it remained wild into the twentieth century and no accurate estimate of the country's moose population was possible. Educated guesses by scientists based on habitat preference and densities from other parts of moose range suggested an estimate at midcentury of 200,000 to 300,000 moose, contrasted to a presettlement estimate of 500,000.

Some provinces maintained records of moose numbers and legal harvests. In New Brunswick, moose began to increase after 1900 and an open season on moose began in 1936. By 1945, game officials estimated 7,720 animals. No province-wide estimates were available during this era for the other Maritime provinces. Nova Scotia's moose were on the rebound at midcentury due in part to a closed season as of 1938. Prince Edward Island may not have had moose by the time Europeans first visited and none were present in 1950. On the island of Newfoundland, moose were not native. A bull and cow were introduced from Nova Scotia in 1878 on the northeast coast at Gander Bay and two bulls and two cows from New Brunswick were introduced near Hawley in interior Newfoundland in 1904. During the first twenty-five years, the descendants of these animals spread rapidly while the population slowly grew. In the next twenty-five years, their numbers increased more rapidly. In 1948, the Chief Game Warden of Newfoundland estimated 20,000 moose in the province.

Quebec's large moose population remained unquantified through the early years of the 1900s. However, anecdotal reports from certain areas and decreasing legal harvests caused concern about the population's fate by 1950.

Ontario's 361,000 square miles represented a daunting challenge for estimating moose numbers. At the start of the twentieth century, moose populations were considered low. In the following years, there was clear evidence of a northwestward expansion and numbers were thought to rise. In the absence of scientific estimates by the provincial Fish and Wildlife Division, the Royal Ontario Museum of Zoology sent out annual questionnaires to specific observers throughout the province. From the results, the Museum suggested that moose numbers were decreasing from 1935 to 1939, increasing from 1940 to 1943, decreasing from 1944 to 1946, and increasing after the hunting season was closed in 1949. Starting in 1949, the Fish and Wildlife Division conducted province-wide inventories annually. For the years 1949 through 1953, the estimate grew steadily from 17,500 to 42,000 moose.

The prairie provinces experienced moose declines throughout the early 1900s, although they did not have accurate estimates of overall populations. Legal kills fell precipitously in Manitoba, Saskatchewan, and Alberta and closed seasons were enacted in the late 1940s in Manitoba and Saskatchewan.

In British Columbia, moose populations were increasing in the 1900s as animals were seen occupying territories in which they had not been seen since settlement. By the late 1940s, there were heavy harvests occurring in the province and game officials there expressed no concern about the herd's ability to withstand the hunting pressure. No scientific population estimates were made, but in 1952, the total population was ventured to be 50,000 moose.

The Yukon and Northwest Territories' immense size and sparse populations of people limited the extent of knowledge of the suspected large moose populations. Despite low numbers of residents, both provinces had high legal kills throughout the middle of the century.

The status of moose populations in North America by 1950 varied across the continent. In places where they seemed to be declining, protection afforded by closed or limited hunting seasons contributed to modest increases. The stage was set for a remarkable and largely unforeseen recovery of moose populations by the end of the century.

Reintroductions

The latter half of the twentieth century has been an important period for some species of wildlife. A number of animals have been brought back from low numbers to become important game animals and aesthetically valued creatures. Wild turkeys, beavers, fishers, river otters, bald eagles, peregrine falcons, and elk are but a few. The moose story is not as well known as some others, but the recovery of their populations has been nothing short of remarkable.

Moose populations have rebounded on their own in some places, but humans have influenced moose recovery in several areas. Attempts at moose recovery started in the late 1800s, but with the exception of the releases in Newfoundland, all met with limited success or failure.

In Nova Scotia, moose were nearly extirpated from Cape Breton Island and in 1928 and 1929, seven moose from the mainland were released there. That attempt failed and in 1947 and 1948, eighteen moose from Alberta were released in Cape Breton Highland National Park. This venture succeeded and there is a small, but stable, population on the island today. In fact, moose on the Nova Scotia mainland are considered to be in trouble and no hunting has occurred there since 1981, while the Cape Breton Island moose population of approximately 3,000 sustains a small legal harvest each year.

In Massachusetts, moose were considered gone by the late 1800s. Six moose from Manitoba were released on a game preserve in the Berkshire hills around 1900. Ten years later, after the preserve was sold, a few moose escaped when the fence deteriorated. These animals held on for at least ten years, but the Massachusetts moose herd never grew.

In 1978, the first moose reintroduction effort to meet with success in the United States started in a modest way in Colorado. On March 3 of that year, a dozen moose in the Bear River area of Utah were captured, using tranquilizer darts. The moose were translocated by helicopter to sites in north-central Colorado where that state hoped to start its own moose herd. The next year, twelve more animals were brought in from Wyoming. In the ensuing eight years, the original herd grew from twenty-four animals to around 250 despite the known loss of forty moose from poaching. In 1987, another group of twelve from Wyoming were released north of Rocky Mountain National Park to establish another herd. From 1991 to 1993, 106 moose from the northern Colorado herd, from northeast Utah, and from southwest Wyoming were translocated to the Upper Rio Grande river basin in southwestern Colorado by the Colorado Division of Wildlife. In 1996, the population had grown to 600 animals in four separate herds.

Michigan had a long history of moose occupying Isle Royale National Park, but those moose were too far from the mainland to provide a source of immigrants for the rest of the state. So, in 1985, the state traded wild turkeys to Ontario for moose. In 1985 and 1987, Michigan released a total of sixty-one moose that had been captured and transported from Ontario's Algonquin Provincial Park where moose are abundant. All moose were released west of Marquette in the Upper Peninsula.

The translocation of moose is an exciting and complicated event. Teams of pilots, drivers, veterinarians, and wildlife biologists work together in a coordinated fashion to efficiently capture, immobilize, and transport the animals—all the time keeping the safety of the moose the highest priority.

Moose were successfully reintroduced to Newfoundland, Michigan, Utah, and Colorado.

Dubbed Moose Drop I and II, the Michigan reintroduction efforts involved all of this. The first of the moose was captured on January 22, 1985. A pilot and wildlife veterinarian in a helicopter flew into Algonquin Park and began looking for moose near lakes. The pilot, who was experienced in herding moose from the air, was successful in moving moose out onto lakes about 75 percent of the time. Once a moose was on the frozen lake, the helicopter approached to within 30 feet and the veterinarian fired a tranquilizer dart into the large hind leg muscle of the moose. The moose typically tried to run back into the forest, but the pilot kept the helicopter between the moose and the mainland. After five to ten minutes, the tranquilizing drug took effect and the moose lay down on the ice.

As soon as the moose was immobilized and the helicopter was landing, the veterinarian radioed a second crew in another helicopter, which consisted of four men and a pilot experienced in hauling cargo. The veterinarian prepared the moose for transport while the second crew flew in. This included applying ointment to the eyes so they would not dry out, a blindfold to keep the moose calm, and ear plugs to muffle the noise of the helicopter during flight.

Upon arrival, the second crew quickly arranged a sling apparatus and got the moose on top of it. Then, they attached the sling to

OVERLEAF: The remains of a moose lie next to a wilderness lake.

113

Moose are now a common sight in areas where they were recently absent.

a sixty-foot-long cargo strap hanging below the helicopter. After ensuring that the sling was properly fastened, the helicopter flew to the staging area, anywhere from one to ten miles away, depending on the capture site. The moose was suspended about 700 feet above the ground and was flown at speeds up to 50 mph, which got it to the staging area in no more than fifteen minutes.

The staging area was the scene of hurried activity. The still-drugged moose was slowly lowered to the ground where a crew carefully folded its legs underneath it to prevent injury. Other veterinarians monitored vital signs, injected the moose with drugs to prevent infection, to eliminate internal and external parasites, and to reduce the probability that the animal would be overly stressed from the

capture. They also took blood samples, checked cow moose for pregnancy, collected fecal samples to check for parasites, and completed an international health certificate. At the same time, other members of the ground crew took measurements, put numbered and colored metal ear tags in both ears, and put a radio collar designed to detect death around the moose's neck.

The moose was then put into a large wooden crate with hay for bedding and loaded onto a truck where it waited for other moose to be brought in. At that time, it was given the antagonist drug to the immobilizing drug, which brought it out of its stupor, and the earplugs and blindfold were removed. Snow was put into the crate so it could be eaten to prevent dehydration. A truckload of one to

Moose recovery in Michigan was accomplished with helicopters.

four moose was then driven 550 miles across the international border at Sault Ste. Marie to the release site in the western Upper Peninsula of Michigan not far from Marquette. The driving trip took seventeen hours.

At the Michigan release site, the crates were unloaded by crane and a veterinarian checked the moose for general conditions. The door to the crate was then opened and the moose released into the wilds of Michigan. Another veterinarian in a helicopter radiotracked each moose for two days after release and biologists periodically radiotracked the moose from small aircraft.

The 1985 release herd was composed of 10 adult bulls and 19 adult cows. In 1987, an additional 15 bulls and 15 cows were translo-

cated and released to make the herd grow more quickly.

The overall release population has grown from 47 moose in the first summer after the release to 378 total moose in the summer of 1995. Moose have spread across the western Upper Peninsula and some have even wandered into northeastern Wisconsin.

The moose release in the western Upper Peninsula appeared to pay dividends for the small remnant population of moose in the eastern U.P. There has been only one record of a release animal wandering east, but the eastern population has grown to around 150 animals recently. That increase is thought to be the result of less poaching, which in turn may have been affected by the positive effects of

Moose came back on their own over most of their range.

back slowly, gradually expanding their range and their numbers until the frequency of observations by people made it evident that moose were on their way back.

State and provincial wildlife agencies spend little of their scant annual appropriations on population surveys of animals that are not regularly hunted or trapped or are listed as threatened or endangered. Thus, the return of moose not only went mostly unheralded, but largely unquantified.

The causes of the comeback are generally speculative and probably involve a complex set of factors interacting at the same time. Controlled hunting and complete protection certainly reduced mortality rates, but how much is questionable. Likewise, the absence of large predators, primarily wolves, in some parts of moose range no doubt took away one more problem for moose. However, it seems more likely that the main causes were related to changes in habitat, climate, and reduced densities of deer.

White-tailed deer populations in the Northeast in the 1960s, 1970s, and 1980s were subjected to a series of bitterly cold winters, which caused high levels of mortality and eventual declines in overall numbers. As deer densities declined, the incidence of parasitic brainworm carried harmlessly by them may have decreased just enough to allow moose to move into areas formerly occupied by deer. In addition, dramatic increases in clear-cutting, particularly softwood forests that provide deer thermal cover in the winter, both helped moose and harmed deer. The deer lost cover. The moose, less dependent on winter cover, gained a new food supply as young trees grew in the cutover areas. The size of clear-cuts also favored moose. On commercially owned timber lands in much of northern Maine, clear-cuts were hundreds of acres in size. While deer and moose both find nutritional food in regenerating forests, deer

the media campaign and the widespread community effort to restore moose to the state.

Other states have considered the possibility of reintroducing moose to augment small and slowly growing populations. Moose reappeared in New York around 1980 and showed signs of becoming a permanent population. In 1990, officials from the New York State Department of Environmental Conservation began to consider translocating moose to a fourteen-county area in the northern third of the state. Based on public comments, however, the State decided to let moose find their way back into New York at their own pace.

Natural Comebacks

Moose populations have generally regained ground on their own with little direct help from humans except closed or controlled hunting seasons. Moose came

Young moose are an indication of growing populations.

prefer smaller openings so that they are never too far from protective cover. Moose, on the other hand, do not have the same behavioral barriers to wandering out into the middle of an expansive cutover. Deeper snow in larger cutovers also prevents deer from utilizing them as efficiently as the long-legged moose.

The concurrent rebound of beavers throughout much of the same range may have played a significant role in the moose comeback, although it would be difficult to demonstrate a direct cause-and-effect relationship. Nonetheless, it seems reasonable to think that the pond habitat created by beaver dams favored moose since they rely on aquatic plants for specific nutritional requirements during the summer months.

As the twentieth century closes, naturally occurring moose population increases have resulted in reasonably secure herds across most of the lower 48 United States and in almost all of the former moose range in Canada. Maine's population has skyrocketed from a meager 2,500 at midcentury to twelve times that at present. During the same period, New Hampshire's moose population may have grown a hundredfold from around 50 to nearly 6,000. Spillover from Maine, New Hampshire, and Quebec has resulted in a population of nearly 2,000 in Vermont and around 50 in New York. In the last twenty years in Massachusetts, the state has moved from an area with frequently seen dispersers to a permanent herd of around 200 moose including some successfully reproducing cows.

In the American Midwest, only Minnesota and North Dakota have experienced natural comebacks. Minnesota's herd grew to over 10,000 animals and North Dakota went from a handful to around 1,500. Wisconsin is the odd state out despite having an abundance of publicly owned land where moose would find potentially suitable habitat. Current thinking

Moose commonly cross icy cold water of winter streams.

suggests that Wisconsin's large northern deer herd may not allow moose to overcome the deleterious effects of brainworm. However, that has not prevented the return of moose in other eastern states with deer.

There may be another element at play in Wisconsin; that is, the position of the state relative to other moose range. Lying on the south side of Lake Superior, Wisconsin is not contiguous with any moose range in Minnesota, and the big lake prevents dispersal of moose from Ontario. Occasional wanderers from Michigan's small herd and a few from Minnesota may be keeping Wisconsin's moose herd at 50 or fewer, but until the Michigan herd starts to expand rapidly or Minnesota's moose range stretches farther south or moose are reintroduced, Wisconsin will not likely have a viable population of moose.

Montana and Wyoming registered the largest gains since midcentury. Montana's

The recovery of beavers has resulted in additional moose habitat.

Canada's moose population numbers nearly one million.

moose herd is nearly 4,000 and Wyoming has over 15,000 moose. Utah's moose population is limited by suitable habitat, but it has remained fairly steady at around 3,000. In Idaho, rapid gains were made in the 1980s and 1990s. Augmented slightly by the relocation of "problem" moose by the Idaho Department of Fish and Game, it wasn't until 1990 that the State had a reasonably accurate estimate of 5,500 moose. Washington is not considered a good state for moose based on the available habitat, but moose have been able to carve out a niche and bring their population to around 300. Moose have never reinvaded what limited range may exist in Oregon. Alaska's moose herd climbed back to around 175,000 animals, which nearly doubles the total for all of the rest of the country.

Across Canada, the natural comeback has resulted in a nationwide moose population of around 800,000 which may approximate the numbers present before European settlement. From Labrador to the Northwest Territories, Canada has reclaimed its moose. The estimated moose populations in the East include 3,000 in Nova Scotia, 2,000 in Labrador, 23,000 in New Brunswick, 65,000 in Quebec, and 125,000 animals from the release herd in Newfoundland. Central Canada has 32,000 or so in Manitoba, 57,000 in Saskatchewan, 118,000 in Alberta, and over 120,000 in Ontario. Western Canada includes 50,000 moose in the Yukon Territory, 157,000 in British Columbia, and around 26,000 in the Northwest Territories.

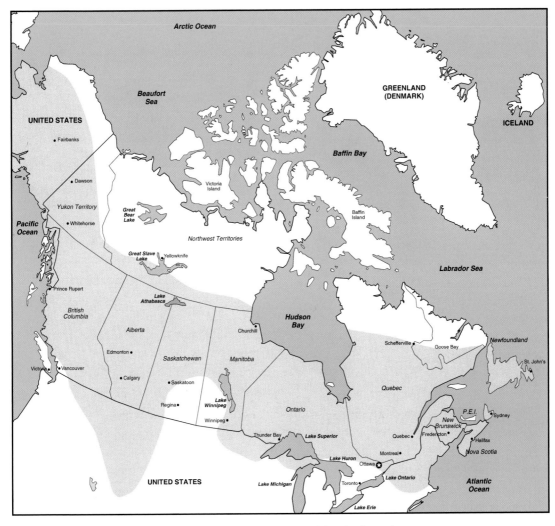

Distribution of moose in North America

Distribution of moose in Eurasia

Moose Around the World

Outside of North America, moose occupy a vast range of environmental and social conditions. Rapid population growth in China, intensive forestry in Scandinavia, the removal of native forests in eastern Europe, and the disbandment of the former Soviet Union have all affected moose populations.

Norway

Norway's moose population is large and well distributed throughout the country. The estimated 125,000 moose live almost everywhere below the treeline, although during summer, some moose wander above the treeline in southern Norway. On the outer central part of the west coast and in the coastal areas in Finnmark, the northernmost county, the numbers of moose are very low. Hunting is not allowed in either area. Also, some larger islands along the western and northern coast have not yet been colonized by moose, but this may only be a matter of time since the moose has been expanding its distribution in Norway during the last fifty years.

There are written records of moose in Norway back into the 1200s and 1300s. For many years, moose hunting was restricted to nobility and poaching was severely punished. In the 1600s and 1700s, the moose population across Scandinavia declined markedly from unknown causes. Heavy hunting by the rural population reduced moose numbers across the country in the 1800s. Moose populations were widespread, but very limited, in the early 1900s. Since the 1930s, they have been on the rise in Norway. The population estimate in 1966 was 40,000 moose and numbers peaked around 1990. A national program for monitoring the population of moose in Norway began in 1991.

Harvests of moose increased at this time and were responsible for starting a modest population decline. The national annual harvest peaked at 39,000 in 1993. In 1996, hunters took 34,100 moose and each year, wildlife officials estimate that harvests account for about 30 percent of the pre-hunt population. This suggests an estimate of a little over 100,000 moose in Norway.

Sweden

Sweden's moose population followed a pattern similar to Norway's until recently. Moose were present across Sweden in low, but stable, numbers historically. In 1789, an edict gave hunting rights to commoners who owned taxable land, resulting in heavy hunting. Unregulated hunting nearly caused the extermination of moose in many parts of the country by 1825.

Completely closed hunting seasons for a ten-year period gave the population a chance to recover. Later, when hunting seasons were reopened, the season was limited to August through November, which eliminated the overly effective hunting on cross-country skis. Moose numbers remained relatively low until the 1930s when the population started to grow rapidly. It grew so fast during the 1970s that in the early 1980s, Sweden's moose population hit what might have been an all-time high at approximately 300,000. At that level, the thriving moose population resulted in numerous motor vehicle accidents and damage to commercial forests.

Wildlife officials used intensive legal hunting to bring the skyrocketing population under control. Through the 1980s and 1990s, heavy hunting pressure has reduced the population to a more acceptable level.

Currently, moose are found throughout Sweden except at the very southern tip toward Denmark and on the island off Gotland in the Baltic Sea. Lowest densities are found in the south. The current overall population is estimated at around 200,000. Intensive forestry practices across much of

Moose numbers are at all-time highs across much of Eurasia.

the country keep moose habitat in good shape and the moose population constantly ready to grow. Sweden's moose management strategy is to shoot about half of the late-summer population to keep the population at or near the existing level. The 1996 harvest was 91,079. This was half of the peak harvest in 1982, which was nearly 180,000 moose. Sweden does not issue a limited number of permits for moose hunting. Instead, there are quotas for certain land areas based on the number of moose in those areas and the population goals.

Finland

Compared to the mountains of Norway and the drier forests of Sweden, Finland is a land of low, level plains with extensive and abundant lakes, rivers, and bogs. Moose have been in Finland since the sixteenth century when they ranged across the country. As in Norway and Sweden, moose populations in Finland were relatively low historically and nearly eliminated by 1850. Moose were given protection status between 1868 and 1898 and the population began to recover slowly. Licensed hunting was permitted for the entire country in 1906. After a period of heavy hunting during World War I from 1914 to 1918, partially closed seasons were established and by 1930, the moose population began to grow. By 1933, when total protection was repealed, there were 3,500 moose in Finland. Populations increased gradually with

The reduction of wolf and deer populations aided moose recovery.

two low periods, one during World War II when food shortages led to extensive poaching and in the late 1960s. Nonetheless, by 1970, there were around 40,000 moose in Finland.

The number of moose peaked in the early 1980s at around 100,000 animals with an annual harvest of 55,000, then fell and has stabilized in the 1990s. In 1997, the population was almost 60,000 moose. The 1996 harvest of moose in Finland was 25,817 animals, a decrease of 20 percent from the prior year. The number of hunting permits issued annually is around 17,000. Each permit allows the hunter to take one adult or two calves. Objectives for moose densities are designed to keep moose within a certain range of numbers for each moose management unit.

Across Scandinavia, moose populations were favored after 1850 by several events. One was the reduction of large predators, namely wolves and brown bears. By the mid-1900s, these predators were nearly absent from the region, although bears have staged a mild comeback. Weather patterns also helped moose. During the past hundred years, climate change in the North Atlantic has resulted in less severe winters and increased precipitation in the summer. A period of warm weather in the 1930s also lowered snow depth and shortened winters, which appeared to have increased survival of calves and unborn fetuses. The change from rural farming to modern forestry decreased the number of domestic animals that were kept in the forest during the summer and that competed with moose for the same food. The increase in clear-cutting of forests, which results in excellent moose food several years after the cut, has created a constant new food supply.

Russia

The vastness of Russia provides ample moose habitat. Historically, moose were abundant in northeastern Russia—the area known as Siberia—until the beginning of the nineteenth century when moose numbers declined and their distribution shrank to the west. In the later 1800s and early 1900s, moose moved back to the east and south. A decline in moose numbers in midcentury ended around 1970 followed by a period of rapidly growing populations until 1985. Moose moved into areas of eastern Siberia where they had been absent for many years including territory near the Bering Sea. They were transplanted onto the Kamchatka peninsula where they still exist today. Moose populations in Siberia are large, but moose occur at fairly low densities across the region except in far northeastern Siberia.

Siberian moose populations were carefully managed using hunting as a tool until 1985 when the dissolution of the Soviet Union began. Following perestroika, there was a period of three to five years of uncontrolled hunting with exceptionally high quotas fueled by the opening of the former Soviet republic to foreign hunters. These hunters were willing to pay large sums of money for the opportunity to shoot a trophy bull with large palmate antlers, the kind that doesn't exist in the rest of Eurasia.

The heavy hunting pressure disturbed balanced sex ratios of bulls and cows resulting in more older cows, a higher proportion of barren cows, and fewer calves. In some areas, the decline was so severe that all moose hunting has been prohibited.

In western Russia, moose occur in higher densities than in Siberia except around cities and human settlements. The vast northern zone of taiga forest with few people is considered a stable area where moose numbers are not exceptionally high but change very little over time. Moose have been present in this area for hundreds of years.

The mixed-forest zone just to the south experiences dramatic changes in moose numbers periodically, including two great depressions in the nineteenth and twentieth centuries. After World War II, when populations were greatly reduced, the moose population started to increase and doubled between 1950 and 1963. Moose numbers in this region of prime habitat can be quite high.

The forest-steppe zone even farther south is inhabited by unstable populations of moose, which disappear from time to time for long periods. Immigrants from the taiga forest region repopulate the two southern regions after declines. After occupying this area in the seventeenth and eighteenth centuries, moose were gone from the southern region in the 1800s, but started to reappear in the 1900s. Currently, moose are relatively common in the two southern regions and reach as far south as the area between the Black and Caspian seas near Georgia and Azerbaijan.

Russian biologists foresee a decline of moose numbers at the beginning of the twenty-first century because of the breakdown in controlled management that has occurred following perestroika and extensive subsistence hunting by people. By the middle of the next century, barring any unforeseen major ecological or social events, they expect eastern Russia's moose population to be recovered and growing.

Ukraine

The land of Ukraine is a vast, flat plain with few hills. Most of the original vegetation has been cleared and few forests remain. Ukraine is at the southern edge of moose range in eastern Europe. Nonetheless, moose occur in high densities in the country. During the 1970s while Ukraine was still part of the Soviet Union, moose numbers fluctuated between 12,000 and 18,000 animals. Current numbers of moose are not readily available.

Latvia

Latvia is characterized by low, flat land with numerous lakes, rivers, marshes, and peat bogs. Forests occupy nearly one-half of the landscape. Much of Latvia was prime moose habitat and their numbers had recovered after World War II to approximately 45,000 animals by 1975. To reduce forest damage, the government initiated a drastic population reduction program through legalized sport hunting and lowered the numbers to 17,000 by 1989. In 1995, the population was approximately 8,700 and one year later was 7,200. Hunters take around 1,700 moose per year although the allowable harvest is not always reached.

Lithuania

Lithuania is characterized by low, flat terrain with numerous lakes, rivers, and wetlands. Forests occupy about one-fourth of the land. Moose were once widespread in Lithuania. Social strife caused by wars resulted in decimation of numerous wildlife populations in the country and perhaps only 300 moose were left after the end of World War II. Five years later, the population nearly blinked out when wildlife officials estimated only 90 moose. However, the reduction of wolf populations, antipoaching efforts, and winter feeding activities resulted in a growing moose population in the 1960s and 1970s. By 1960, there were 1,100 moose and the population leaped to 7,400 by 1970. In 1973, there were 10,000 moose and numbers fluctuated between 7,000 and 15,000 for the next two decades.

At that level, moose were inflicting substantial damage to forests and to agricultural lands. Legalized hunting increased in the 1970s and 1980s with 1,500 to 3,200 moose harvested each year, and moose populations stabilized. By 1990, the population was 6,900. After 1991, intensive hunting and poaching sharply reduced moose numbers. In 1993, the population was cut in half to 3,400 and by 1996, only 3,000 remained. Annual legal harvest was only 85. In 1997, Lithuania's moose population stood at 3,800 animals. Moose were found across the country with most of the population in the northeastern districts.

Belarus

Belarus is a country of the former Soviet Union and lies in eastern Europe. The land is primarily a low-lying plain with hilly uplands and numerous lakes and rivers. There is a vast tract of uninhabited swampland in the southern part of the country. Forests cover nearly a third of the land. Like other countries in eastern Europe, Belarus lost many of its moose during the two World Wars, but after the mid-1940s, moose populations increased quickly. During the 1970s, moose numbers fluctuated between 22,000 and 29,000. Densities of moose in Belarus were among the highest in Eurasia. There is little information about moose in Belarus at present due to the dissolution of the former Soviet Union and the establishment of a new government.

Moose live primarily in national parks and other refuges in central Europe.

Poland

Moose once occupied a large part of Poland, but were decimated in the first half of the twentieth century from the combined effects of two world wars, poaching, and changes in the national borders that took away Poland's best moose habitat. In 1937, only 1,130 moose occurred in Poland. World War II threatened the existence of moose in the country and moose were protected from hunting after the war. Numbers of moose were as low as 425 in 1965. An intensive reintroduction program and immigration from the Soviet Union resulted in rapid gains in the population, and hunting was resumed in 1967. By 1975, there were 3,250 moose and in 1981, the population was over 6,000 animals. Polish wildlife officials increased hunting pressure to reduce the herd, which was causing extensive damage to Poland's remaining forests.

Currently, the country's approximately 5,000 moose are restricted almost entirely to primeval forests of national parks, landscape parks, and other wild, protected areas in the northeastern and eastern parts of the country. Two of the best places for moose in Poland are Biebrza National Park, a large area of peatlands preserved in its natural condition in northeastern Poland and Bialowieza National Park and Primeval Forest, a unique lowland woodlands. Moose are absent from

the western part of the country and around the Baltic Sea in the northwest, as they are from the Carpathian Mountains in the southern part of Poland.

The present status of moose in Poland is thought to be secure with the ongoing establishment of nature preserves. Hunting is the primary means of population control. Game management is conducted by over 60,000 nonprofessional hunters organized in several thousand hunting clubs. Each club leases one or more of the 5,000 hunting districts. Hunters not only harvest animals, but are required to conduct annual habitat improvement programs and population censuses.

Estonia

The land of Estonia is low, with numerous lakes, rivers, and wetlands. Wetlands and lakes comprise a quarter of the country and forests cover another quarter. Moose range over most of the forested regions. During the 1970s, Estonia's moose population fluctuated between 7,000 and 11,000 animals. In 1991, biologists estimated 13,000 to 14,000 moose, but just five years later, the population had dropped by 50 percent. The harvest quota of 7,000 and kill of 6,400 in 1991 had been reduced to 1,300 and 2,000 by 1995. There is extensive poaching in the country as well as significant predation by bears and wolves. Wildlife officials are trying to regulate legal and illegal hunting to allow the population to stabilize or increase. In 1997, Estonia's moose population seemed stable at around 6,500.

Kazakhstan

Kazakhstan is mostly low lying with mountain ranges in the central and southern parts of the country. Deserts and semideserts

make up two-thirds of the land. Only 4 percent of the land is forested.

Kazakhstan is at the southern limit of moose populations in central Asia. Historically, populations fluctuated as they did for moose in other southern regions. In 1975, as moose were reclaiming areas from which they had been absent, there were an estimated 1,300 moose in the country. Today, moose have repopulated their entire historic range in the country as well as some areas without records of prior habitation.

Biologists have identified three populations of moose. In western Kazakhstan, there are approximately 600 moose. The forest-steppe regions of northern and northeastern Kazakhstan support about 1,700 moose. The eastern part of the country has approximately 1,300 moose. In the last ten years, the population has decreased from 5,500 to 3,600. The overall decline is primarily attributable to a decrease in the eastern population of 1,700 animals. Moose have been hunted legally since 1972 and 200 to 250 moose are killed annually.

Mongolia

Mongolia is home to both the Siberian and Manchurian subspecies of moose. Both are considered very rare and have been protected through a closed hunting season since 1953. The total moose population in the country is estimated at 11,000. The Siberian moose is found in northern provinces along the border with Russia. It lives in taiga zones along river valleys and is occasionally seen on high mountain plateaus in summer. Its range is estimated at 6,500 square miles. The Manchurian moose is at the western edge of its distribution in Mongolia, occurring in only a few river basins and low hills in the far

Russia holds the bulk of Asia's moose, as Canada does for North America.

131

As the twentieth century closes, moose are secure over most of their range.

eastern provinces in a 6-square-mile area. Its numbers in the country do not exceed 100. Illegal hunting and predation by wolves are thought to keep the moose population low.

China

China is home to the Manchurian moose. At the beginning of the nineteenth century, moose were found throughout northeastern China in Manchuria. The population was apparently very large. Hunting was common by inhabitants of this sparsely settled region. Since that time, moose range has shrunk northward to the northern tip of the Heilongjiang Province. Exploitation of forests, war in the 1940s, and increases in the human population caused moose to fall back into lightly settled forested areas or into Nature Reserves. Today, unlike moose in virtually all other parts of the world, the range of the Manchurian continues to shrink to the north.

Hunting was out of control and poaching was serious during the Cultural Revolution from 1966 to 1976 even though hunting was forbidden in 1973. The first official moose census in 1976 revealed about 18,000 moose and was considered to be the lowest point in recent history. Moose populations grew in the 1980s partially recovering the losses of the prior twenty years.

Today, moose are abundant only in the northern and western parts of their small range in China. Approximately 70 percent of the moose live there. Areas to the east and south have three separate moose populations, each of which has fewer than 500 individuals. The overall population is decreasing. Forest cover in moose range in Manchuria has shrunk from 70 percent of the land area a hundred years ago to half that today.

China's burgeoning human population and their intensive exploitation of natural resources threaten the moose's future. Chinese government officials have taken steps to protect their remaining moose including the establishment of five nature reserves and the planning of three others. In 1989, the Wildlife Conservation Law was passed, which legally protected moose. Today, hunting is allowed only by a special permit from the provincial government.

CHAPTER EIGHT

The Moose in a World of People

Moose were the source of food, clothing, and tools for aboriginal people and early settlers of northern regions of the world. Today, moose are important to some people as subsistence, but the majority of people prize moose as a potential recreational experience and as a sport-hunting trophy. Burgeoning moose populations in areas also densely populated by humans have resulted in increasing numbers of vehicular accidents and other undesirable interactions between moose and people. Because moose eat so much food on a daily basis, they can change the vegetation significantly when their populations are dense. Damage from browsing has been a concern of landowners trying to raise a crop of trees for their commercial value.

Moose conservation is complicated in today's social environment. The conflict between people who value sport hunting and those who don't affects how government wildlife officials manage the herds in their areas. Human safety concerns people who have had a brush with a moose on a road while those who have never been in moose country don't understand. The effects of moose on commercially valuable forests are felt keenly by some and are unappreciated by others. Against this backdrop, professional wildlife managers continue to monitor and study moose populations, to provide opportunities for sport hunting, to manage limited amounts of moose habitat, to minimize damage caused by moose, and to provide wildlife viewing opportunities on public and private lands.

Abundant moose populations lead to numerous moose-vehicle collisions.

The moose provides food and utilitarian items for native peoples.

Moose in Native Cultures

The moose has been an important creature in the cultures of the first inhabitants of North America, the people who crossed the Bering land bridge between Siberia and Alaska and settled the western hemisphere. Not surprisingly, moose were the focus of some woodland Native American cultures in the boreal forest region much as plains Native American culture revolved around the buffalo and coastal Inuit cultures rose and fell with seals and whales. Throughout present-day Canada and the northern United States, a variety of tribes found great utility in the largest package of walking food in the forest.

Cree, Ojibway, Algonquin, Iriquois, and other tribes relied on moose before the coming of Europeans. Today, some tribes retain, through long-held treaties, the right to hunt, fish, and gather in areas they ceded to federal governments. In Minnesota, for example, tribal hunters from the Fond du Lac band of Lake Superior Chippewas, from tribes that are part of the 1854 Treaty Authority, and from the White Earth band of Minnesota Chippewa Indians harvest moose during the state hunting season. In Maine, the Passamaquoddy and Penobscot Indian Nations administer moose hunts and take about a hundred animals annually. Cree Indians in northern Ontario and Quebec have long-standing traditions of moose hunting and practice their own forms of moose conservation based on their understanding of Nature.

In the northern part of the Northwest Territories, the Gwich'in First Nations people settled a land claim in 1994 with Canada creating the Gwich'in Settlement Area. Moose are at their northern limit in this far northern land and reach densities of only one moose per 4 square miles, but they have become an important subsistence animal for these people, especially when caribou numbers are low.

Alaska has the greatest number of native people reliant on moose for part of their daily life. In Alaska, moose were not present in many regions of the state until the last hundred years and some native people did not have a history of moose in their culture. The Koyukuk people who occupy an area in the central part of the state have lived in that area for thousands of years, but the moose has become an important part of their way of life only since its arrival around the late 1800s. For the Koyukuk people, the postglacial colonization of North America by moose changed their entire way of life. As Richard Nelson wrote in his book, *Make Prayers to the Raven*, "Indeed, it must have seemed like a miracle to the elders when they saw this great animal slowly spreading into the Koyukuk tributaries and down the wildlands around their settlements. Few events could have been more fortuitous. But in a world where change is the rule, no one would assume that the moose could not disappear again."

The Moose as a Game Animal

Today, sport hunting is the focus of moose management across most of the animal's range. The art of moose hunting attracts the imagination of adventurous outdoorsmen. A bull moose with a large set of antlers is a highly coveted prize, and the sev-

eral hundred pounds of meat may be the source of protein for an entire family for a year. Moose hunting also provides economic opportunities for local guides, outfitters, and sporting camps in wild moose country.

Traditional use of moose as big-game animals has been challenged in some areas. The debates over whether or not to reestablish moose hunting seasons in Maine and New Hampshire after those states experienced dramatic comebacks in moose numbers attracted national attention and debate. Subsistence hunting by indigenous peoples in Alaska, Canada, and the lower 48 United States has proven controversial despite reserved treaty rights or legislated rights.

Currently, moose can be hunted legally in twelve states and eleven provinces as well as in most Eurasian countries where they exist. All of the states and provinces offer resident hunting permits; seven of the twelve states and all of the provinces offer nonresidents an opportunity to hunt moose. Michigan does not currently offer moose hunting opportunities, but is expected to do so in perhaps the next few years as the moose population continues to increase.

Hunters eager to find a place to hunt moose have a variety of ways to obtain a moose hunting permit. In Canada, many provinces offer over-the-counter licenses to whoever cares to purchase one. Parts of some provinces have a limited quota of permits for specific hunting areas and use a lottery system to determine the permittees. There are permit quotas and open license sales in different parts of the same province in a few provinces.

Alaska offers moose hunting permits in a system similar to that of most Canadian provinces. The smaller moose populations in the lower 48 United States require more careful management and only a limited number of moose licenses are given out each year. Each state has a slightly different system, but they all use some type of lottery.

Differing objectives for managing moose result in dramatically different moose hunt strategies. High levels of damage to commercial forests and of vehicle accidents have led Scandinavian countries to harvest a large proportion of their moose annually, nearly 50 percent in some years. Despite having only 600 moose, Colorado officials allow a tightly controlled hunt of just a few animals a year to provide a big-game hunting opportunity. In the Yukon Territory, only around 1 percent of the annual population is harvested due in most part to the inaccessibility of the terrain.

Hunter success rates vary greatly from year to year and across moose hunting territory on the continent. In general, however, hunters in the lower 48 enjoy the greatest success, achieving rates near 100 percent in states with few permits, to an average of 80 or 90 percent in states with larger moose populations and more permits. In Canada, there is a greater variation. The general rule of thumb there is that hunters using an outfitter achieve a much higher success rate than those hunting on their own.

In general, moose populations are harvested fairly lightly, although there is great variation among states and provinces. In areas with high human populations and where moose-viewing opportunities are equally important to the public, the harvest tends to be lighter. In places where moose are problems or cause damage, the harvest is higher.

The Maine Moose Hunting Controversy

Moose hunting has not received total support from people living in the areas. States with a long tradition of moose hunting and those in which hunting is a widely accepted practice have not had much controversy. In Maine, the proposal to hunt moose after many decades of not doing so stirred fierce debates, from the halls of the state legislature to backwoods taverns. I was a graduate student at the University of Maine pursuing a Ph.D. in wildlife ecology when the great debate over opening a moose hunting season made the state the focus of media attention for a number of months.

The first law to protect moose in Maine was passed by the state legislature in 1830 and shortened the season to a period September through December. Additional laws were passed further restricting moose hunting until 1935 when the last hunting season for many years was held in three south-central coastal counties. Increased moose populations renewed interest in moose hunting, and in 1943, a bill was introduced to restore moose hunting. It was defeated, as was a similar bill in 1951 and annual bills from 1957 to 1977. In 1977, both the State House of Representatives and Senate passed a moose hunting bill, but it was vetoed by the governor. In 1979, a bill passed in both houses and was signed into law by a different governor. It authorized a hunt of 700 moose in 1980 by resident hunters in a section of northern Maine north of the Canadian Pacific railroad line. During that hunt, 636 moose were killed.

The passage of the moose hunting bill into law did not occur without a fight. In the state legislature, lawmakers engaged in bitter debates over the idea. Outside the Legislature, antihunting individuals and groups and others who supported hunting in general but opposed the moose season were organizing and protesting.

The drawing to determine who would be one of the permittees was called "Moose Tuesday." The 32,927 postcards from applicants were transported in a state police van

Moose hunting is popular but controversial in some areas.

and were guarded by two state troopers and two state game wardens. The three-hour drawing was broadcast on television, and press from around the country attended. The event produced one of the largest audiences for a public television show in the history of the state.

The first season was covered widely by television and other media. The flames of dissent were fanned as moose unaccustomed to being the prey of humans displayed little wariness and were shot on roads and other highly visible locations.

A number of dissenters formed a group calling itself SMOOSA (Save Maine's Only Original State Animal). It ran public ad campaigns in newspapers and on television and radio. In the meantime, the state legislature overwhelmingly passed another law providing for annual moose seasons beginning in 1982. SMOOSA was able to gather enough signatures on a petition, however, to force a public referendum that would determine the future of moose hunting in Maine.

In response to SMOOSA's efforts, proponents of moose hunting organized and began running their own ad campaign. The efforts of proponents helped defeat the referendum vote in November, 1993, when 60 percent of the voters supported continuation of the hunt. Since that time, Mainers have come to accept and embrace moose hunting, but many regret the days when moose roamed the woods of Maine with no fear of man.

Moose viewing can be done in areas with spectacular backdrops.

commuters into the city and by moose to get away from heavy snow in the nearby foothills. Following the lead of British conservationists who built tunnels under highways for frogs and toads to use, Alaskans built a ten-foot-high tunnel under the highway in hopes of reducing the number of accidents. Although few moose were observed using the tunnel at first, the number of accidents reported the first year was less than half of the yearly average. Lights were installed along seven miles of the highway and a two-mile section of fence was erected near the tunnel to guide the animals to the preferred crossing area.

Alaska and New Hampshire have even instituted programs of public education to warn motorists about the danger of hitting moose.

Concern for Public Safety

The extensive network of paved roads and the ever-increasing number of vehicles on them traveling at ever-increasing speeds pose a problem for wildlife and for people.

People driving in moose country know that a brush with a deer is a weak cousin to a collision with a moose. Weighing five to ten times more than a deer, a moose often causes as much damage as it receives.

Sweden has a larger number of moose-vehicle collisions than any other area. Sweden has used fencing and roadside clearing in many areas and has been successful in reducing collisions.

In some places where accidents with moose are particularly common, special measures are taken to reduce them. In Alaska, around 40 moose per year were killed on an eight-mile stretch of the Glenn Highway north of Anchorage. The highway is used by

Moose Watching and Celebration

Though not as orchestrated as whale-watching expeditions or bird-watching trips, thousands of people garner great enjoyment from simply looking at moose. Over much of their range, moose are readily visible from highway vehicles and show no great fear of man. It was the moose's tameness that opponents to newly created moose hunting seasons in states like Maine and New Hampshire feared would disappear, and with it the opportunity to sit on the shoulder of a road and watch a moose grazing or dunking its head in a pond.

The translocation of moose from Ontario to Michigan provided an opportunity to see how much interest people would have in viewing moose. The translocation effort itself attracted wide public attention and support, and many people were interested in seeing the moose after they were released. In 1990, the Marquette County Convention and Visitors Bureau categorized all of the informational

Shallow ponds are the best areas in which to find a moose in summer.

inquiries it had received and found that moose were the second most frequently asked about, behind only waterfalls. This prompted the Bureau to produce the pamphlet "Moose Locator Guide," with a map of six auto tours on which a moose sighting is highly likely. Over 20,000 copies of the pamphlet are distributed annually.

Moose are so abundant and popular in some places that local communities have developed celebrations around them. Alaska's Kenai Peninsula harbors one of the highest moose populations in North America. People come from all over the world to the Kenai National Wildlife Refuge to see these famous Alaska moose. In Talkeetna, Alaska, residents put on the Moose Dropping Festival. Attendees are encouraged to bring the dried moose feces they collected the previous winter. Alaska is one of the few places in the world where you can buy a necklace of moose pellets strung on a rawhide cord or a paperweight made from varnished moose pellets.

What better place to have a celebration of moose than in Greenville, Maine, on the shores of Moosehead Lake. The Moosehead Lake Region Chamber of Commerce sponsors a month-long MooseMania celebration in May and June. Events include the Moose River canoe race, Tour de Moose mountain bike race, Moosehead Lake Rowing Regatta, and hikes to favorite moose-watching spots.

Though not as well known as the calls of the loon or other wildlife, the sounds moose make are quite familiar to people living in wild moose country. And moose-calling contests have become very popular all across North America.

Nuisance Moose

Not only have moose numbers increased dramatically over the last half century, but moose have also moved closer to cities and

Moose calves are most easily viewed with their mothers.

towns. One result has been an increased incidence of nuisance moose that are likely to either hurt themselves or damage property and people.

In many areas, moose wander into town and cause traffic problems and damage to property. This is particularly common in Anchorage, Alaska, where moose killed by vehicles number over 200 annually and where wayward moose stomped two people to death in recent years. From a management standpoint, these events are far from humorous and often present wildlife and law-enforcement agencies with a "no-win" set of conditions.

On one hand, large animals weighing over a ton and sporting large antlers and powerful hooves are a serious public safety concern when they are in and around people. On the other hand, most people want the animal to be removed safely with no harm done

As moose populations grow, they are seen more frequently in towns.

to it. Wildlife officials in many states and provinces are able to tranquilize moose for relocation, but this is risky and expensive. Moose tranquilized in an urban setting are under a great deal of physiological stress and the tranquilizing drugs can have unpredictable effects. In some cases, moose can't be safely captured and wildlife managers are forced to kill the offending animals. Wildlife officials have proposed moose hunts in and around cities with chronic moose problems—they have met with expected controversy.

One nuisance moose found its way into the hearts of many people in 1986. That fall, in Shrewsbury, Vermont, a 700-pound young bull moose, obviously confused about its own mating season, took up with a Hereford cow named Jessica on a farm. For seventy-six days, he faithfully attended the cow until his antlers fell off and he lost his interest in mating. He wandered off in the woods and was not seen again.

Other moose have been seen consorting more persistently with cattle. In 1985, a bull attended twenty heifers on a farm in upstate New York until it became such a nuisance that it was tranquilized and relocated fifty miles away. The next summer the moose was seen a mile from the farm and in the fall rejoined the farmer's herd. This time, the bull was taken even farther away, only to show up the next spring in a nearby farmer's cattle herd.

Motorists are warned in areas where moose cross roads frequently.

Moose as Damage Agents

The effects of moose browsing are readily visible in many parts of moose range. Eating 50 pounds of twigs a day during the winter, a moose is like a giant hedge trimmer in a thicket of willows and may eat as much as 85 percent of the new growth put on by willow shrubs in a given year.

The effects of moose browsing across a broader scale are less apparent, but moose produce some significant changes to the forests in which they live. High degrees of browsing in some areas have led forest managers to be concerned about the effects of browsing on the commercial value of forests.

In Wyoming, moose thrive in some areas that also support ranching operations. The winter range of these moose herds is in the willow thickets of riparian zones along rivers. These areas have a high percentage of private ownership and are often in grazing land or hayfields. Ranchers typically cut and store hay outside for winter cattle feed. When the hay includes a high percentage of alfalfa, moose frequently eat all or some of the bales and stacks, and ranchers file complaints with the Wyoming Fish and Game Commission. The Commission has tried to prevent damage in specific areas by providing wintering moose with their own alfalfa. This has helped to a limited degree and has been augmented by increased hunting

A moose's keen senses let it detect people before being seen.

opportunities in those areas.

Supplemental feeding has also been tried in Scandinavia where there can be significant economic loss in Scots pine and Norway spruce forests and in agricultural fields. In Finland, wildlife officials and farmers develop cultivated fields with highly desirable moose foods in an attempt to keep moose out of nearby agricultural areas. Also in Finland, salt stones have been used to attract moose to specific parts of forests where they end up heavily browsing the trees. The idea is to concentrate the damage to specific areas instead of having moose damage extensive areas.

Supplemental feeding has also been tested as a way to pull moose through severe winters, especially in areas where people and moose live in close proximity. The winter of 1989-1990 was such a winter on Alaska's Kenai Peninsula and in the Matanuska-Susitna Valley. The numbers of starving moose and those killed by trains and automobiles as the moose tried to feed in rights-of-way brought a public outcry to feed the moose. This prompted state officials to test different kinds of winter feed and to debate the usefulness of such a program. In studies conducted on captive moose, locally grown hay and pelleted rations were found to provide enough nutrition to keep moose in relatively good condition for three winter months. While it is unlikely that supplemental feeding of moose will ever be widely used, it remains an option for specific situations.

Predator Reduction

Since the settling of North America, killing of predators such as wolves, mountain lions, bears, and coyotes has been a standard practice largely justified in the name of protection of domestic livestock. As sport hunting became widely popular and generated revenue for local governments, predator control shifted its focus to reduction of predation on species such as white-tailed deer, elk, caribou, and moose. All along, wildlife agencies operated under the assumption that predators controlled the number of their prey, therefore, fewer predators meant more game animals.

In his classic essay, "Thinking Like a Mountain," well-known author and conservationist Aldo

Leopold started to shatter that well-accepted myth. In the last few decades, the commonly held belief that predators like wolves control their prey populations has now been largely abandoned in the scientific community for a far more sophisticated set of principles that recognize the natural complexities of ecosystems, of which individual predator and prey species are just parts. The notion, however, has not been so quickly abandoned by the general public, and particularly by some segments of the hunting public. Despite advances in the scientific understanding of predator-prey interrelationships, there have been recent efforts to increase moose populations by simply reducing the number of predators. Most of these efforts have occurred in Alaska where large populations of big-game species attract hunters from all over the world and where substantial populations of large predators still roam.

Alaska has a long history of killing predators, particularly wolves, in the name of maintaining large herds of moose and caribou. Moose populations in part of central Alaska increased after a wolf-reduction program in the 1950s and reached their peak abundance in the 1960s. The correlation between predator control and increased moose numbers was not missed by many Alaskans—including politicians, who instigated further wolf-control measures in the 1970s. Those aerial hunting activities were the focus of a national controversy over the ethics and efficacy of the role of predator control in managing game populations.

Shooting and trapping wolves in Alaska has been common. Up until 1971, anyone could shoot wolves from an airplane or helicopter in the state, but that year, the U.S. Congress passed the Airborne Hunting Act, which limited the use of aircraft for hunting wolves. The state allowed "land and shoot" programs for a number of years and carried

out wolf-control programs on its own until 1992 when the Department of Fish and Game moved to reauthorize and re-fund scientific wolf control. This proposal created a national debate. Then–Governor Walter Hickel received thousands of letters, telephone calls, and faxes from people all over the world who opposed the proposed hunt. Alaska's tourism department projected a loss in state revenues of $85 million if the hunt occurred. The planned start-up date was postponed in late 1992 and, in January of 1993, a "wolf summit" was held in Fairbanks in an effort to find a constructive solution to the problem.

Despite the work of the Alaska Wolf Management Planning Team, which produced a document that had a consensus recommendation for wolf-management goals and objectives including use of aerial wolf-control methods only as a last resort, Governor Hickel and the Alaska Board of Game approved aerial killing of wolves in some areas to allow moose and other game animals to increase. In 1994, Hickel signed into law a bill which directed the State Department of Fish and Game to manage for specific levels of certain game species including moose. This bill was lobbied against by the National Audubon Society and other conservation organizations.

Tony Knowles became governor in late 1994 and soon after being sworn in in 1995, he met with officials from the Alaska Department of Fish and Game, representatives from the National Audubon Society, and other groups to discuss aerial wolf killing. Soon afterward, he issued an Executive Order which ended the activity. In all, approximately 200 wolves were killed in the two years before the moratorium.

Since that time, the wolf hunting controversy in Alaska continues. In November of 1996, voters approved by a 58 to 41 percent

Predator control has been used to increase calf survival.

keep moose and other ungulate populations high remains uncertain.

In the Yukon Territory of Canada, provincial wildlife officials are concerned about the low numbers of moose and caribou in the Aishihik region of the province. Instead of hunting wolves, they are experimenting with a wolf sterilization program. Wolves are shot with a tranquilizing drug from a helicopter and transported to a nearby veterinary clinic where both males and females are sterilized. Their idea is that a pair of wolves can still occupy and defend its territory from other wolves and that reductions in wolf numbers will occur through lack of births to the sterilized pairs. The program is not without its critics, mostly from the urban centers of Canada, and has widened a rift between urban dwellers and rural residents who depend in part on wild game for their subsistence.

Managing Moose Habitat

Wildlife management agencies have spent relatively little effort on improving habitat for moose. Moose populations have generally recovered as the result of landscape changes out of the control of wildlife agencies and other factors working in concert. Nonetheless, public land management agencies in some areas conduct timber harvest activities with moose in mind.

In the Superior National Forest in northeastern Minnesota, moose and white-tailed deer range overlap. In an effort to favor moose over deer in parts of the Forest, wildlife biologists recommend larger-than-average clear-cuts that minimize the total amount of area within 400 feet of the edge of the harvest area. Both moose and deer prefer young trees and shrubs that sprout in cutover or burned areas. This method relies on the behavioral differences between moose and deer. Deer prefer smaller, more linear clear-cuts because they are less comfortable

margin a law that prohibits the landing of an airplane and shooting of a wolf on the same day by hunters. That law went into effect in late February 1997. Nor can the state conduct aerial wolf control unless the Commissioner of Fish and Game makes written findings that a biological emergency exists and that wolf control is the only feasible means of addressing the emergency.

Just months earlier, the State of Alaska commissioned the National Academy of Sciences to conduct a study of the economic and scientific bases of state wolf and brown bear control programs. The results of the study released in October 1997 indicated that past studies were not designed in such a way to determine the long-term effectiveness of predator control, nor did they include analyses necessary to determine whether the programs helped wildlife or benefited the state's economy. The future of wolf management to feeding far away from cover. Moose, on the other hand, venture more readily into large open areas. This pattern is particularly evident in areas where both moose and deer are preyed upon by wolves, but not so obvious in areas where deer have little to fear from predation.

Like deer, moose typically feed closer to the edges of clear-cut areas. Wildlife officials in Ontario have evaluated moose use of different shapes of clear-cuts and have found that heaviest utilization by moose occurs in harvest areas that are within one hundred feet of an edge. However, it appears that moose are more limited to edge areas during the winter when snow depths require them to stay close to dense conifer forests, which accumulate relatively little snow. They use up too much energy walking through deep snow typically found in clear-cut areas.

Moose habitat has been manipulated in Ontario, Quebec, and other places to lessen the effect of hunter pressure. In areas that are heavily hunted because of numerous access roads, wildlife managers often encourage timber operations to leave uncut blocks of timber in a checkerboard pattern to provide moose with refuge areas where they are not so vulnerable to hunting. In tests conducted in the late 1980s, researchers from the Ontario Ministry of Natural Resources found that moose populations in block-cut areas were much higher after hunting than those in nearby continuous cutover areas. The size of the blocks was associated with moose use; the larger the uncut block, the more use by moose.

Studying Moose

The current understanding of moose biology and ecology, and the sophisticated management of moose and moose hunters would not be possible without the past and ongoing

Moose have responded well to logging, which has created young forests.

efforts of moose researchers and wildlife managers. Far too numerous to mention, these dedicated professionals provide the questions and answers to the most important moose conservation issues.

Moose have become important enough to many people that moose research centers have been established. Perhaps the most well known is the Moose Research Center in Soldotna, Alaska, on the Kenai Peninsula. Located next to the Moose River Flats calving area on the Kenai National Wildlife Refuge (formerly known as the Kenai National Moose Range), this center has been functional since 1968 and the work done there has resulted in hundreds of publications and reports and substantial knowledge about moose.

Moose research and management has evolved with changes in scientific methods and technologies. Today, wildlife managers use aircraft and satellites to monitor moose numbers. Computer systems keep track of permits and important management data. Some moose wear radio collars or collars fitted with state-of-the-art Global Positioning System hardware. Researchers use new DNA and other genetic methods and ultrasound technology to probe deeper into moose ecology.

In this day and age of computerized and electronic gadgetry, Dr. Joel Berger of the University of Nevada–Reno is using observation, mimicry, and a strong right arm to aid his research efforts. Berger is interested in how moose, which have not had wolf and bear predators around for over a hundred years and dozens of moose generations, will respond when the predators come back. He has been studying the moose in Grand Teton National Park, Wyoming, which will likely be meeting up with wolves and grizzly bears soon. The wolves and bears are expanding their ranges south from Yellowstone National Park.

To test the moose's responses to these predators, Berger has provided stimuli to their sense of hearing and smell. He plays tape recordings of wolf howls and has found that the Grand Teton moose seem unfazed, unlike the response from a control group of moose in Alaska. However, his tests of smell have provided different results. He and his wife wear a two-person moose suit. In the moose suit, they slowly approach feeding moose until they are close enough for Berger to throw snowballs of either wolf feces and urine or bear feces and urine close to the moose. Again, the moose seem unconcerned by the wolf scent, but change their feeding pattern in response to the bear scent. The results of his studies won't be known for several years and, by then, the first wolves or bears in the area may have made their first moose kills.

Moose populations have been heading in the right direction.

The future for the moose is secure.

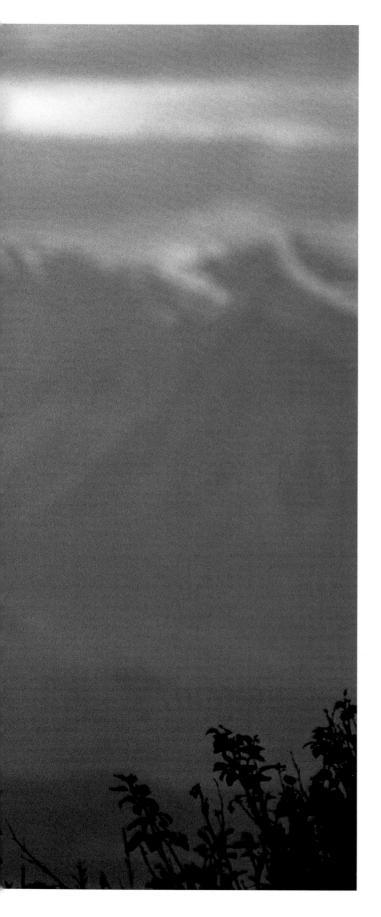

Afterword

There is reason to think that moose will be around for a very long time. Unlike other creatures that have had their habitats and numbers reduced by human activity, moose populations have responded positively to many of the changes people make.

Much of moose country remains wild as we approach the twenty-first century, and trends in human expansion into and use of these vast areas seem unlikely to change drastically. Eventually, moose may find themselves with too many human neighbors, but that scenario will only occur in localized areas in the foreseeable future.

For now, the moose is secure. Much less secure are the ecosystems that support moose, humans, and a host of other organisms. The boreal forest itself is not disappearing, but the forces that shaped it and its inhabitants have changed. Natural fires are largely suppressed. Logging changes landscape patterns and the composition of plant communities. Aboriginal peoples and their ways of life have been reduced to remnants of the past. Sulfur dioxide air pollution alters the composition and function of lakes and forests.

Like the loon, wolf, and other north country denizens, the moose's future will be largely determined by its ability to continue to modify its behavior in response to an ever-changing environment and by the desire of humans to retain some wild moose country.

Appendix

The following population sizes are estimates based on a variety of methods used by state and provincial wildlife management agencies and usually reflect a post-hunt midwinter population.

The figures presented are estimates for 1997. There has been no official estimate for Idaho from the Idaho Department of Fish and Game since 1990 when 5,500 moose were thought to occur in the state. Populations in Idaho have increased dramatically since the mid-1980s based on numbers of sightings and other anecdotal evidence.

State / Province	Population
Alaska	175,000
Alberta	118,000
British Columbia	175,000
Colorado	600
Idaho	—
Labrador	2,000
Maine	30,000
Manitoba	32,000
Massachusetts	200
Michigan	1,100
Minnesota	10,290
Montana	4,000
New Brunswick	23,000
Newfoundland	125,000
New Hampshire	6,000
New York	50
North Dakota	1,500
Northwest Territories	26,000
Nova Scotia	3,000
Ontario	120,000
Quebec	65,200
Saskatchewan	57,000
Utah	2,700
Vermont	2,000
Washington	300
Wyoming	15,100
Yukon Territory	63,564

Further Reading

The moose is one of the most studied and written-about wild mammals in the world. There is no shortage of scientific and popular articles for the intense or casual reader. A few are listed here.

Randolph L. Peterson. 1955. *North American Moose.* University of Toronto Press, 265 pp.

Douglas B. Houston. 1968. *The Shiras Moose in Jackson Hole, Wyoming.* Grand Teton Natural History Association Technical Bulletin 1:1-110.

Albert W. Franzmann and Charles C. Schwartz, editors. 1997. *Ecology and Management of the North American Moose.* Smithsonian Institution Press, Washington, D.C., 640 pp.

Rolf O. Peterson. 1977. *Wolf Ecology and Prey Relationships on Isle Royale.* National Park Service Scientific Monograph Series Number 11.

Rolf O. Peterson. 1995. *The Wolves of Isle Royale: A Broken Balance.* Willow Creek Press, Minocqua, Wis., 190 pp.

Alces, The journal of the North American Moose Society, Lakehead University, Thunder Bay, Ontario.

Moose Call Newsletter, an official publication of the *Alces* journal.

Index